ASPECTS OF LANCASTER

Aspects of Lancaster

DISCOVERING LOCAL HISTORY

Edited by
Sue Wilson

Series Editor
Brian Elliott

Wharncliffe Books

First Published in 2002 by
Wharncliffe Books
an imprint of
**Pen and Sword Books Limited,
47 Church Street, Barnsley,
South Yorkshire. S70 2AS**

*For up-to-date information on other titles produced under the
Wharncliffe imprint, please telephone or write to:*

> **Wharncliffe Books
> FREEPOST
> 47 Church Street
> Barnsley
> South Yorkshire S70 2BR
> Telephone (24 hours): 01226 - 734555**

ISBN: 1-871647-95-9

A CIP catalogue record of this book is available from the
British Library

Cover illustration: *China Lane, Lancaster.* Courtesy of Lancaster Libraries

Printed in the United Kingdom by
CPI UK

CONTENTS

INTRODUCTION .... *Susan Wilson* **6**

1. LANCASTER CASTLE AND THE FATE OF THE
   PENDLE WITCHES .... *Susan Wilson* **7**

2. CATHOLICISM IN LANCASTER
   AND DISTRICT .... *Norman Gardner and Tony Noble* **13**

3. THE QUAY TO SUCCESS: DEVELOPING
   AN EIGHTEENTH CENTURY PORT .... *Peter Williamson* **27**

4. THE RISE AND FALL OF THE STAINED
   GLASS TRADE IN NINETEENTH CENTURY
   LANCASTER .... *Suzanne Boutin* **41**

5. THE LANCASTER DOCTORS:
   THREE CASE STUDIES .... *George Howson* **53**

6. THE FOUNDING OF GREAVES
   METHODIST CHURCH .... *Lois M R Louden* **63**

7. THE DUKE'S THEATRE .... *Bernard Gladstone* **75**

8. A SPIRITED LEAP INTO THE UNKNOWN ..... *Graham K Dugdale* **85**

9. SOME WATER-POWER SITES IN THE
   LANCASTER AREA .... *P J Hudson* **99**

10. THE GRANDEST MONUMENT IN
    ENGLAND .... *Mike Whalley* **115**

11. FROM CONFINEMENT TO COMMUNITY:
    THE STORY OF 'THE MOOR', LANCASTER'S
    COUNTY LUNATIC ASYLUM .... *Peter Williamson* **123**

12. LIBRARIES OF LANCASTER .... *Michael Margerison* **139**

CONTRIBUTORS **153**

INDEX **159**

INTRODUCTION

by *Susan Wilson*

'FROM MORECAMBE BAY AND ACROSS to the Cumbrian Hills'. This phrase opens *Aspects of Lancaster*. It is fitting because Lancaster is a historic town surrounded by a seaside resort and the wonderful countryside of the Lake District. The castle that is the focus of Susan Wilson's article is also right in the centre of Lancaster. The building, like the town, is steeped in history. Many notable events have happened over the centuries at the castle, not least the famous trial of the so-called Pendle Witches, one of many court proceedings to be held in our county town. Lancaster has its fair share of supernatural stories and ghostly tales, and Graham Dugdale recounts for us some most interesting examples.

Lancaster, and its neighbourhood also posses a deep religious history; Norman Gardner and Tony Noble's article points towards the empathy that has long existed in our locality for Catholicism. The stately spire of St Peter's Cathedral has long been a prominent feature of the skyline, opposite the castle and the priory. Methodism has also flourished in and around Lancaster, as has the earlier religious movement known as the Religious Society of Friends or the Quakers as they became commonly known. Lois Louden's chapter on the Greaves Church demonstrates the strong Methodist feeling in the town, whilst several other articles refer to the key influence of the Quakers. Even Bernard Gladstone's article on the Duke's theatre provides an unusual insight on an aspect of Lancaster's religious history.

Industry and commerce played important roles in the growth of Lancaster to the present day. The splendid eighteenth century buildings along the Quay provide unmistakable visual evidence of commercial development, a theme discussed by Peter Williamson in his essay on Lancaster as a port. Suzanne Boutin's article on stained glass also reminds us of our artistic and manufacturing heritage. Another reminder of local agrarian and industrial history is Phillip Hudson's interesting and detailed contribution on water-powered sites.

No history of Lancaster would be complete without some reference to Lord Ashton. The majestic memorial that rises above Williamson's Park, gifted by Ashton to his native city, is the subject of Mike Whalley's fascinating chapter which also gives us some insight into the man behind the edifice. Close by, is what was the Moor Hospital. The impressive building once played an integral role in Lancaster's social history, serving as the County Lunatic Asylum. Its story is outlined by another contribution from Peter Williamson. A medical theme is also investigated by George Howson who explores several case-histories of Lancaster's medical pioneers. Michael Margerison discusses the growth of the public library movement in Lancaster, providing us with yet another aspect of our social and community history.

Lancaster has a diverse and varied history and *Aspects of Lancaster* attempts to bring the reader a glimpse of its rich cultural heritage.

1. LANCASTER CASTLE AND THE FATE OF THE PENDLE WITCHES

by Susan Wilson

MORECAMBE BAY TO THE CUMBRIA FELLS and back along the River Lune. This is the view that the eye can take in from Lancaster Castle (Figure 1). The castle is the most important building in Lancaster's long history. However, for such an important and strategic building, there is a certain amount of mystery surrounding the dates of its earliest history.

It is thought that a local tribe, the Brigantes, first set up a rough kind of Roman fort on the hill above the Lune. It was a natural look-out point, and there were several springs and a well so that defenders would always have their own fresh water supply. One of these wells still stands in the basement of the Well Tower.

Roger of Poitou, the son of William the Conqueror's cousin, and a loyal supporter of William's Conquest of England, was awarded lands between the River Mersey and Furness in thanks for his support. He chose to build on the hill, Cherca-Lon Castrumas, in part because of its natural spring, and founded the Priory Church on that site in 1084, and a few years later built the first Norman motte and bailey castle. After this, the castle belonged to various people, most famously perhaps, to John O' Gaunt who built the gateway tower and endowed the castle with much of its splendour. The castle

Figure 1. Lancaster Castle in 1998. *Author's collection*

also has a great keep, known as the Lungess Tower. John Earl of
Morton built the Gatehouse, and he was also responsible for
enlarging the castle. Indeed, the castle has many different periods of
architecture, although Saxon and Gothic are the prevailing styles.

As well as being a fortress, Lancaster Castle has also served as a Gaol
since 1585. Indeed, it is the oldest prison building in use in England,
and many people have been tried and hung there over the years. Until
1799, the accused were taken out to Lancaster Moor and executed in
public; after this date, hangings took place in the castle grounds, but
they were still a public spectacle. In 1536, many were imprisoned
following the Pilgrimage of Grace, an uprising against Henry VIII and
his religious changes. Most famous among these, was John Paslew, the
Abbot of Whalley Abbey in Lancashire. Similarly, following the
Jacobite Rebellions against George I in 1715 and against George II in
1745, Lancaster Castle again played host to many of the captured. A
number of the imprisoned, like the Catholic priest James Swarbrick,
died in the castle before coming to trial. In 1652, the nonconformist
George Fox had a vision on Pendle Hill, which led him to found the
Quaker movement. Fox's refusal to take the Oath of Allegiance to
Charles II meant that he too was imprisoned in Lancaster Castle.

In later years, Lancaster Castle served as a debtors' prison. In 1837
it is no surprise to find a record of 320 debtors held there. The castle
was also used to house people categorised as 'lunatics', until the law
was changed in 1816. Right up until the twentieth century, the castle
has been used to hold those who were imprisoned due to their
'unusual behaviour'. This was the case with Edward Harley, hanged
for being a wizard, and also for the Pendle Witches.

Although the Pendle Witch story is a much written about topic, it
is still shrouded in mystery. Perhaps one of the most authentic books
about the trial is *A Wonderful Discoverie of Witches*, by Thomas Potts,
written only a year after the trial, in 1613. This book provides the
official story. It was written at a time when belief in witches and
witchcraft was commonplace. Moreover, the Gunpowder Plot of
1605 had created a general air of suspicion about things that were
perceived to be unusual. Witchcraft was seen by many to be the
survival of an ancient religion. Doctors were expensive at this time,
and many instead turned to 'wise women'. The prevailing attitude of
the time was that hardship was a reflection of ungodliness.

The Pendle Witch saga revolves around two families, both of which
were led by old women. Demdike was almost blind and lived with her
widowed daughter, Elizabeth Device and her three children, Alizon,
James and Jennet. Chattox, so called because she was always muttering

and chattering to herself, was really called Anne Whittle, and she lived with her daughters Elizabeth and Anne. Anne married a Thomas Redfearn. Although the trial itself took place in 1612, it is the incidents that led up to it which created fear in peoples' minds. Demdike's home was broken into, for example, and clothing and oatmeal were stolen. Elizabeth Chattox was later seen by Alizon, Demdike's daughter, wearing a cap stolen from Demdike, and it was eventually agreed that Chattox was to pay a yearly tribute of meal, and that she would do no more harm. However, after some years, the tribute ceased to be paid and Demdike was reduced to life as a beggar. Another incident took place in 1590, involving a Christopher Nutter, who was travelling home from Burnley with his sons Robert and John. Robert fell ill, and felt his illness to be linked to Chattox, as Chattox lived on the Nutters' land, and Robert Nutter had tried unsuccessfully to seduce Anne Redfearn. When Anne Redfearn repulsed him, he had vowed revenge, and banished Anne and her family from their home. Robert, a retainer for Sir Robert Shuttleworth of Gawthorpe Hall, went on a tour of Wales with his work, and never returned. He died, accusing Chattox and her daughter to the end.

In 1660, ten years after the Nutter incident, Demdike's daughter, Elizabeth, asked her mother to appeal to her employer for higher wages. The employer, a local miller called Richard Baldwin, refused, and it seems that Demdike may have replied to this with a curse. It may have been forgotten, had not the miller's daughter become ill and died. This was probably not a rare occurrence in these days of primitive sanitation and hygiene, but the stories were never completely forgotten.

The events that really led to the trial of 1612 began with an incident on 18 March of that year. Alizon Device, Chattox's daughter, was returning home after a day's begging, when she met an old pedlar, John Law of Halifax. She asked for some pins, but refused her request. She cursed him, and he fell to the ground, with what we would probably now call a stroke. However, in the early part of the seventeenth century, such an occurrence was immediately perceived to be unnatural, and therefore witchcraft. John Law's son was sent for, and he found Alizon and accused her of bewitching his father. In the end, Alizon confessed and begged forgiveness, and a local magistrate, Roger Nowell of Read Hall, Whalley, was brought in. Alizon was detained by Roger Nowell, eventually telling him about the history of the two families, and sent to Lancaster Castle. Then, on 2 April, Demdike, Chattox and Anne Redfearn were ordered by Nowell to meet him at Fence, the meeting place for Pendle business. Nowell had all three detained, and had them sent to join Alizon in Lancaster Castle.

On 6 April, Good Friday, friends and neighbours gathered at a place called Malkin Tower, and this meeting was to become known as the Great Assembly. James Device had already, by the time the meeting convened, committed a crime. He had stolen sheep in order to feed his family, despite the fact that Good Friday was a day upon which meat was not eaten for religious reasons.

Roger Nowell conducted an enquiry into this Meeting on 27 April. The meeting was said to be a perversion of a Christian festival, and a black sabbath gathering, where plans were allegedly made to blow up Lancaster Castle and free the four already held there.[1] This sensational tale was enough to conjure up memories of the Gunpowder Plot. Moreover, James Device denounced his grandmother, Ann Chattox, for taking human remains from Newchurch in Pendle churchyard, and helping the constable to dig up teeth. Janet Device shopped her own family and others for being present at the Malkin Tower meeting. Alice Nutter was a surprise attendee at the enquiry, a well-to-do woman; she had paused at the Malkin Tower meeting, perhaps passing through on her way from Roughlee to attend Catholic Mass. Elizabeth Device also argued that Alice and she had bewitched a man, Henry Mytton, to death for refusing them money. Alice was eventually bundled off to share a cell with the others in Lancaster Castle.

Roger Nowell sent the Devices to Lancaster Castle, along with Alice Nutter, John and Jane Bulock, Katherine Hewitt and Alice Gray. Alice Gray was eventually to be acquitted. The others at the Malkin Tower meeting probably fled the scene. At Lancaster Castle the Castle governor, Thomas Covell (the Covell Cross outside the Judges Lodgings in Lancaster is a memorial to him) (Figure 2), examined Chattox and James Device. Chattox claimed Demdike had converted her to witchcraft, but Demdike was by now a dying woman and was to die in the Castle never having stood trial.

On 17 August, the trial opened. The judges were Sir Edward Bromley and Sir James Altham. In spite of the complexity of the trial it did not last long. Chattox was the first in the dock, old and bent. She pleaded not guilty, but eventually broke down and confessed all and asked for mercy for her daughter, Anne Redfearn. Elizabeth Device was next, she was charged with murdering three people, John and James Robinson, and Henry Mytton. She admitted these offences, but denied them in court. However, Roger Nowell produced a star witness in Jennet Device who, along with her brother James, went against her own kin and gave evidence against her mother, Elizabeth. Elizabeth then pleaded guilty.

James was next in the dock and had to be dragged into court. He was charged with murdering Anne Townley, and again Jennet was

Figure 2. Covell Cross outside the Judge's Lodgings, January 1975. *Gillian Woodhouse*

brought in to give evidence and secured a conviction. Anne Redfearn was found not guilty of murdering Robert Nutter, but was found guilty of murdering his father. Alice Nutter was accused of the murder of Henry Mytton, and James and Jennet gave written evidence in this case. There was an identity parade for Alice, and it was Jennet that singled Alice out. Katherine Hewitt was convicted of murder after pleading not guilty. John Bulock and his mother Jane, who lived at Moss End Farm near Newchurch, were convicted of turning Jennet Deane mad. They were picked out in an identity parade by Jennet Device. Alizon Device came into the dock to be faced by John Law, the pedlar he was accused of laming. The sight was too much for her, and Alizon fainted, confessing all when she revived. The sight of the pedlar must also have moved the court, for the judges promised that something would be done to provide for him.

In all, ten witches were convicted. They were brought back into court to hear their sentences. The judge ordered them to be hanged on Thursday, 20 August. There is argument as to whether they were hung on Lancaster Moor or in the grounds of the castle, but the event is sure to have been a public spectacle. It can be argued that the witches would more probably have been hung in the grounds of the castle, as the strain of the walk from Pendle to Lancaster Castle, and the ensuing imprisonment and trial may well have rendered the accused in no fit state to move any further. However, many writers favour Lancaster Moor as the place of execution. As with so much else in this story, the exact details are shrouded in mystery.

Two more witches were tried with the Pendle Witches, Isobel Roy and Margaret Pearson. Roy was known as the Witch of Windle, and was tried, found guilty, and sentenced to death by hanging. Pearson, the Padiham Witch, was found guilty, sentenced to imprisonment and the pillory. Jennet Device's family was destroyed at a stroke. However, twenty-one years later she would return to Lancaster.[2] This time she would be on trial for witchcraft. There were more convictions of witches in 1633, but they did not gain the same level of notoriety as the 1612 trial, and the tales were more outlandish.

James I, King at the time of the Pendle Witch Trials, believed strongly in witches and witchcraft. He believed that witches had tried to drown him and his bride, Anne of Denmark, by raising storms at sea. Therefore, he strengthened the existing laws against witchcraft. Roger Nowell had to act against the Pendle group, or he would have risked his position. It was not until 1736 that these witchcraft laws were repealed.

The 'witches' themselves probably had little idea why they were being arrested. They had no one to defend them, and may have been forced to confess in some cases. Their confessions were written down (Figure 3), and copies can be seen in Lancaster Reference Library.

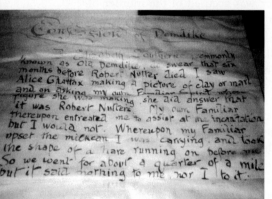

Figure 3. Confession of Demdike.
Author's collection

The Pendle Witches story brings a huge amount of tourist business to the Pendle and Lancaster areas. There is a trail, which starts at Barrowford at the Pendle Heritage Centre and ends after forty-five miles at Lancaster Castle. Many books have been written on the subject, both factual and fiction, proving that the story still elicits interest. Indeed, the Pendle Witch story has proved to be one of the most enduring periods in Lancaster's long history.

Notes and References

1. Harrison, G B, *The Trial of the Lancaster Witches*, 1612.
2. Catlow, Richard, *The Pendle Witches*.

2. CATHOLICISM IN LANCASTER AND DISTRICT

by Norman Gardner and Tony Noble

THE ROMANS BUILT A FORT and a port of Lancaster, but no Christian remains of that period have yet been discovered. The earliest positive evidence of a Christian church unearthed by archaeologists, is St Patrick's Chapel at Heysham Head on the shores of Morecambe Bay (c 900 AD). Other pre-Conquest churches or remains have been found at Heysham, Bolton-le-Sands, Halton, Hornby, Melling and Lancaster (Figure 1) and some of these are displayed in Lancaster Museum and Priory Church.[1]

The Normans radically changed the structure of the church, by re-naming or demolishing some Anglo-Norse churches as at Beetham, and by introducing a new form of monasticism to the area. The Premonstratensians from Croxton Kerial Abbey, Leicester, held

Figure 1. St Patrick's Chapel, Heysham. *Author's collection*

Cockersands Abbey and Hornby Priory as well as the living of the parish of Melling. The dedication to St Wilfrid on two fragments of Anglian crosses (now in Hornby Parish Church) which came from the Priory suggests this was a re-foundation of an unrecognised Anglian monastery. The Furness Abbey Cistercians held fishing rights and land at Lancaster, which were often a source of conflict with Lancaster and Cockersands. The Benedictines arrived at Lancaster priory in 1094, from the house of Seez in Normandy at the invitation of Roger Poitou and occupied a church dating from the Saxon period. A seventh century Anglian cross was found in the churchyard and several other fragments of pre-Norman crosses were discovered when the north wall was moved to house the chapel of the King's Own Royal Lancaster Regiment in 1903. Links with Seez were severed during wars with France in 1414, when it was given to the convent of Syon in Middlesex. The nuns of Syon considerably enlarged and rebuilt it until the death, in 1430, of the Prior (whom the nuns had allowed to stay on). A perpetual vicarage was created on 1 March 1430, Richard Chester was appointed the first vicar and the church became the parish church of Lancaster with a vast parochial area taking in parts of Lunesdale, Wyresdale, and Toxteth Park near Liverpool. From 1260, Dominicans held the Friary which is shown on Speed's map of 1610, and was partly sited on the present site of the Town Hall in Dalton Square. A Franciscan house survived briefly in Lancaster but its location is uncertain. In Leonardgate, a leper hospital was founded c1190 and this was given to the nuns of Seaton in Cumberland in 1355, but it had fallen into ruin by 1531.[2]

The suppression of the monasteries by Henry VIII between 1536 and 1539 removed a vital link in the social fabric of the Lancaster district which resulted in sympathy for the rebellion of 1536 known as the 'Pilgrimage of Grace'. The Abbot of Whalley was executed and two Furness Abbey monks were imprisoned in Lancaster Castle when the rebels disbanded unbeaten, most being pardoned by the King in 1536. Catholic hopes of a reversal of fortune rose with the accession of Mary (1553-58) during whose reign Protestants suffered in the castle. Ultimately, the Catholic cause died with defeat at Culloden in 1746 and the 1766 death of the 'Old Pretender'. However, former monastic lands at Lancaster and Cockersands had been acquired by the Dalton family of Thurnham, before Elizabethan anti-Catholic laws prevented this and during the reign of the Catholic Queen Mary. Despite heavy fines for Recusancy (failure to attend services of the established church), they held twelve acres of land east of Lancaster, the site and grounds of the former Dominican

Figure 2. Martyrs Memorial, Highfield, Lancaster. *Author's collection*

Friarage from 1557. This was leased for development from 1783 by John Dalton (1745-1837) of Thurnham Hall through his agent and architect Edward Batty. The development included the Catholic chapel and school in Dalton Square and Friar's Passage (following the *Relief Act* of 1791). The street names Lucy Street, George Street, Mary Street, Great John Street and Dalton Square refer to family members and Thurnham Street refers to the family estate.[3]

During this 'Dark Age', Recusants (Catholic and Protestant dissenters who refused to attend the established church services), suffered brief periods of bloody terror and long years of suppression and harassment. This imbued in them respect for those who suffered, especially those who were put to death. The execution ground on moorland east of the town was never clearly defined to avoid any martyrs rising, but it is thought it was probably on the site of the old workhouse, now Lancaster Grammar School premises, between Quernmore Road and Wyresdale Road. A modern memorial to all the martyrs of all faiths who died at Lancaster stands nearby on terracing adjoining a recreation ground north of Quernmore Road opposite Williamson Park (Figure 2). The martyrs were not residents of Lancaster district, but many locals were fined and incarcerated in the castle or failing that in lodgings in Lancaster when political conditions made dissenters dangerous, especially in the years 1660,

1678, 1679, and 1682. During the troubled years of Charles II's reign (1660-85) and especially after the Peace of Nijmegen (1678) when the army was not disbanded, many Protestants suspected a Catholic plot to overthrow the government with the aid of French, Irish and Scottish troops. In 1682, Recusants in Lancashire received over 10,000 summonses, of these only 139 were non-Catholics, including seventy-five Quakers. Non-Catholic dissenters were also caught under anti-papist legislation. Papism described everyone thought to sympathise with Catholic beliefs, and was often used as a term of abuse by Protestant sectarians about other Protestant sectarians. These sectarians tended to support a republic on the lines of Oliver Cromwell (1599-1658, interregnum 1653-59), and Catholics who sought a Catholic Stuart king were known as Jacobites. At Lancaster, 471 names are recorded in 1682 including about 235 persons from 43 townships in Lonsdale Hundred, including in the Lancaster district, Arkholme, Ashton cum Stodday, Borwick, Bulk-cum-Aldcliffe, Caton, Claughton, Ellel, Halton-cum-Aughton, Heaton-cum-Oxcliffe, Highfield, Heysham, Hornby-cum-Roeburndale, Lancaster, Leighton, Overton, Poulton Bare and Torrisholme, Quernmore, Scotforth, Bailrigg and Burrow, Silverdale, Tatham-cum-Ireby, Skerton, Scale Hall, Thurnham, Tunstall, Warton, Whittington, Wyresdale, and Yealand. The gentry families of Brockholes at Heaton-cum-Oxcliffe, Middleton at Silverdale, Carus at Halton and Whittington, Dalton at Thurnham are well represented along with numerous husbandmen and small traders of Lonsdale. The gentry at least could pay up in full whilst the poorest paid nothing. Fortunately, the penal laws were often poorly enforced, and in 1680 magistrates at Lancaster petitioned the King to decide on the fate of some £60,000 in recognisances or sureties of £400 per person held against their good behaviour until the Recusant conformed to the established church. In October 1680, the recognisances of those who had failed to appear before the magistrates were paid into the treasury (estreated), but those who had appeared, swore allegiance to the king and agreed to be of good behaviour, did not have their recognisances estreated by the court pending a decision by the king.[4]

The threat of prosecution at any time contributed to a steady trend towards emigration by Catholics, Quakers and others to America and the West Indies. During this period, when the Mass was forbidden, Catholics attended secret meetings to 'say prayers', the code word for Mass, whilst Quakers attended 'conventicles', which were also forbidden, but these terms were loosely used to describe meetings of both faiths. Such centres for Catholics were known as Recusant

Houses. These were located on houses owned by the gentry south and east of the town at Thurnham, Aldcliffe, Dolphinlee, Highfield (near Williamson Park, Lancaster), Quernmore Park, and north of the River Lune at Heaton, Scale Hall and Halton. All were within easy reach by foot or boat from Lancaster. Dolphinlee in particular was an important centre and had a secret hiding place for priests, and a priest was often resident at Aldcliffe. There were, it is known, many 'church papists', who complied with the law concerning attendance at church but maintained their belief in Catholicism. This is shown by analysis of the names confirmed by the Catholic Bishop Leyburn in 1687, when 157 people were confirmed at Aldcliffe and a further eighty-seven at Thurnham. The Jacobite risings of 1715 and 1745 were not widely supported in Lancashire, England's most Catholic County. John Dalton of Thurnham and Albert Hodgson of Leighton were the principal 1715 rebels in the Lancaster area supported by around 100 men, who included a barber and a joiner from Lancaster, local Catholic gentry and their supporters. The Jacobite defeat at Preston on 15 November resulted in a large contingent of prisoners being held at Lancaster Castle. The backlash on peaceful Catholics after both these risings resulted in much suffering and injustice. The resident Recusant priest at Aldcliffe in 1715, Dr Edward Hawarden moved to London and the Caruses at Halton lost their land after the '45. In 1745, the priest Nicholas Skelton was held in Lancaster Castle, when Henry Bracken wrote,

Here is a romish priest ... who gives five or seven pounds a week in clothes and money etc among the rebels he has lived in Lancaster long ... and a large assembly of hearers he had, for this a vile neighbourhood for papists and jacobites.[5]

Once the Protestant succession was assured following the abdication of James II (1689), a slow relaxation of pressures on dissident Protestants by the *Toleration Act* of 1689, was followed by toleration and eventually restoration of Catholic rights to public office and property. Ann Fenwick, née Benison (1724-1777), founded the Hornby Catholic Mission in 1762, eventually replacing the Mass Centre at Robert Hall, Bentham. She obtained in 1770, a landmark decision at the King's Bench which prevented her brother-in-law from taking away her estate on the grounds that a Catholic could not inherit property. Her case was watched by many Catholics with great interest and marked the beginning of the restoration of property and other rights to Catholics. On 3 April 1712, the old Cavalier, Thomas Tyldesley, and his cousin the Reverend W Westby acquired Thomas

Gibson's two houses with a barn to the rear, in St Leonardgate, with the intention of providing a priest's residence. As mentioned above, the priest, Edward Hawarden, lived at Aldcliffe between 1712 and 1715, but from 1715 the Leonardgate houses, (demolished 2000) opposite the Grand Theatre, with a barn used as a Mass centre to the rear, in what later became Mason Street, were occupied by a succession of Catholic priests. Here the Reverend William Winckley resided some time between 1715 and c1720, followed by the Reverend Nicholas Skelton after c1720 or 1740-1766, James Tyrer (1766-1783), Richard Edmondson (1783-1784), and Doctor John Rigby (1784-1818). The former Mass Centre still exists (2000) as part of Nisbett's Knitting factory, having been converted into a row of houses during the nineteenth century and can be viewed from the rear of St Leonard's house. The *Relief Act* of 1791 made lawful the building of Catholic chapels under strict conditions, and after starting a building in modern King Street, Doctor John Rigby was offered a better site, and established the Dalton Square Chapel, which was used for worship between 1799 and 1859. He resided in the house next door which had the first free Catholic school in Lancaster to its rear, in Friar's Passage. The principal subscribers for the new Chapel were the Worswick and Gillow families, Mr Dalton of Thurnham also subscribed along with other members of the congregation, total subscriptions being £975. Sale of the old chapel buildings to Mr Gillow raised another £610 and funds belonging to the mission added £549. Further subscriptions raised the necessary £2,311 7s 0d (£2,311 35p) required. The latter was situated at the Dalton Square end; the entrance being made by a wide square headed door at the north-east corner. The school sited at the north west corner of the chapel was built in 1805 and extended in 1818-20. It was a small building of two stories, the lower one for boys, and the upper one for girls. In 1825 about eighty children attended. Dr Rigby died on 10 June 1818, and it was April 1819 when the Reverend George Brown was appointed, retaining care of the mission until 1841. He was succeeded by his nephew, the Reverend Richard Melchideas Brown, who moved to the new church of St Peter, now the Cathedral (Diocese of Lancaster, founded 1924, formerly Liverpool), when the Dalton Square St Peter's Chapel closed in 1859.[6]

Lancaster was transformed during the eighteenth century from a rural market town to an urbanised industrial centre, despite the decline of its port which had ceased foreign trade by 1810. Research has shown that in 1767, the population in Lancaster was about 3,500 with just under seven per cent of these (236) registered as 'Papists', and the window tax returns of 1766 show that they were evenly spread around the town. Many trades are represented but Catholics had not significantly entered the merchant class at this time. About thirty-three per cent of the Catholics registered were migrants from outside of Lancaster. As the ranks of the surviving Catholic aristocracy and landed gentry, including the Brockholes of Claughton-on-Brock, and the Daltons at Thurnham, thinned, the Calverts of Cockerham and Prestons of Ellel Grange sold their lands in 1774. Late eighteenth century Catholic merchants, like Gillow (c1722), Worswick (the banker, 1794), were followed in the nineteenth century by the Coulston brothers (tanners), Whiteside (banker), Leeming (malster) and Preston (tanner), who built up a Catholic gentry based on trade to replace the patronage of the landed gentry. Some of the earliest rural chapels in the vicinity of Lancaster were funded by Lancaster merchants like Gillow of Leighton Hall at Yealand Conyers (1782). As mentioned above, Hornby was founded by Anne Fenwick in 1762, although its most distinguished priest and historian, Dr John Lingard (1771-1851) complained of the decline of his congregation which had removed to industrial centres in and around Lancaster during his tenure. Scorton (1713) received support from the non-Catholic Duke of Hamilton, who had industrial and landed interests and a powerful voice at the highest levels of government. Thurnham (1785) was assisted by the absentee Calverts, Prestons and Daltons who held the former friarage lands in Lancaster which increased in value as Lancaster expanded. Garstang, long a strong centre of recusancy, obtained its chapel in 1778, sending its minister as a rising priest to serve the congregations of the Fylde. Map 1 on page twenty shows ancient sites, eighteenth century chapels and recusant prayer houses. Map 2 on page 21 shows Catholic and other sites in Lancaster.[7]

The nineteenth century Catholic population of Lancaster swelled by demographic increase (some families had more than thirteen children), and by immigration, as rural and textile manufacturing and water-powered industries like the complexes at Caton and Halton declined. Rural industry found itself unable to compete with Lancaster's strategic advantages of canal, railways, short sea connections, and steam-powered industry with an insatiable appetite for low skilled mill hands, which expanded during the nineteenth century. Lancaster's Irish population was relatively small, although many worked in the County Mental Hospital (construction began c1850), similar institutions and also as teachers in Catholic schools.

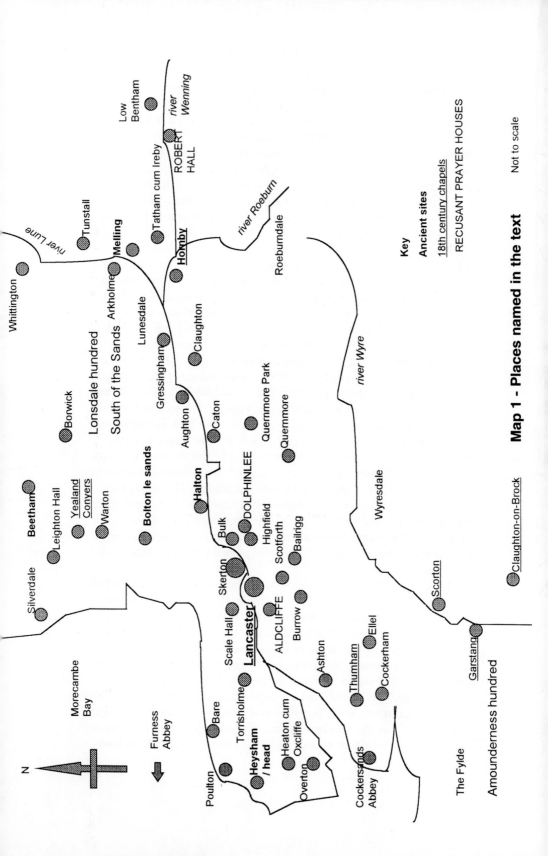

Map 1 - Places named in the text

Key

Ancient sites

18th century chapels

RECUSANT PRAYER HOUSES

Not to scale

N

Morecambe Bay

Furness Abbey

river Lune

Whittington

Silverdale

Beetham

Leighton Hall

Yealand Conyers

Warton

Borwick

Lonsdale hundred

South of the Sands

Tunstall

Melling

Arkholme

Lunesdale

Gressingham

Claughton

Low Bentham

river Wenning

Tatham cum Ireby

ROBERT HALL

Hornby

river Roeburn

Roeburndale

Aughton

Caton

Quernmore Park

Quernmore

Bolton le sands

Halton

DOLPHINLEE

Bulk

Highfield

Scotforth

Bailrigg

river Wyre

Wyresdale

Poulton

Bare

Torrisholme

Scale Hall

Skerton

Lancaster

ALDCLIFFE

Burrow

Heaton cum Oxcliffe

Heysham / head

Overton

Ashton

Thurnham

Ellel

Cockerham

Cockersands Abbey

Scorton

Garstang

Claughton-on-Brock

The Fylde

Amounderness hundred

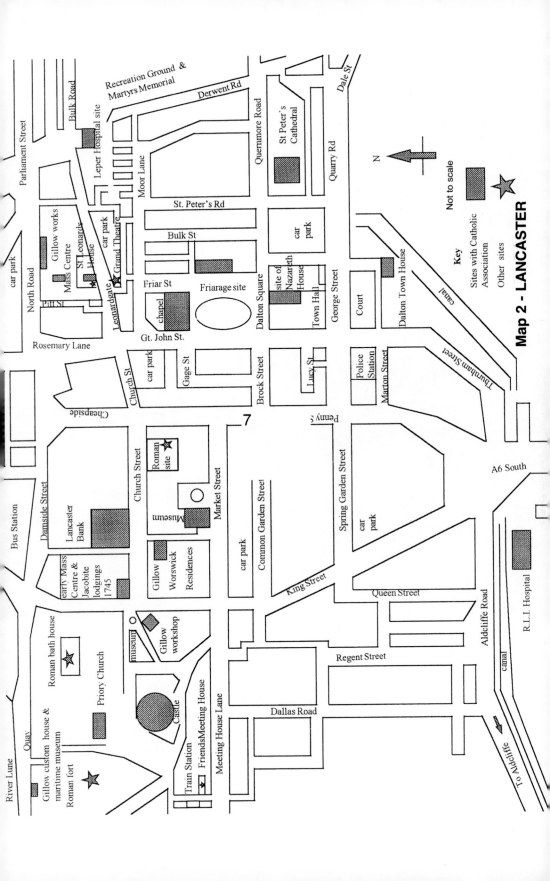

Map 2 - LANCASTER

Not to scale

Key

★ Sites with Catholic Association
☆ Other sites

Recreation Ground & Martyrs Memorial

Derwent Rd

Dale St

St Peter's Cathedral

Quarry Rd

Quernmore Road

Leper Hospital site

Moor Lane

Bulk Road

Parliament Street

St. Peter's Rd

car park

Gillow works

Mass Centre

St Leonards House

car park

Grand Theatre

Bulk St

car park

Dalton Town House

Thurnham Street

canal

North Road

Pitt St

Leonardgate

Friar St

Friarage site

site of Nazareth House

George Street

Court

Marton Street

chapel

Dalton Square

Town Hall

Rosemary Lane

Gt. John St.

Church St

car park

Gage St

Brock Street

Lucy St

Police Station

Penny's

Cheapside

7

Church Street

Roman site

Market Street

Common Garden Street

Spring Garden Street

car park

A6 South

Damside Street

Lancaster Bank

Museum

car park

King Street

Queen Street

Aldcliffe Road

R.L.I. Hospital

Bus Station

early Mass Centre & Jacobite lodgings 1745

Gillow Worswick Residences

Regent Street

museum

Gillow workshop

Roman bath house

Priory Church

Friends Meeting House

Meeting House Lane

Dallas Road

canal

To Aldcliffe

River Lune

Quay

Gillow custom house & maritime museum

Roman fort

Castle

Train Station

N

Figure 3. Priory Church, Lancaster. *Author's collection*

However, the sea links to Lancaster were via Glasson Dock (opened 1826) to Liverpool, and this suffered from competition from Preston's improved port facilities after 1846, and it was 1849 before the North Western Railway reached a jetty at Morecambe, which tended to carry iron ore from Ulverston. The Irish Famine (1845-51) stimulated Irish farmers to produce meat and dairy produce which was shipped via the Mersey, further reducing Lancaster's coastal trade. Many Catholics who came via Liverpool and Preston to Lancaster were second generation Irish, born or raised in England. Many of these families have provided priests for the Lancaster diocese and elsewhere, but other English families like the Coulstons of Roeburndale and Lancaster, also provided priests and nuns, as well as churches and schools.[8]

The loss to Lancaster's faithful Roman Catholics of a beautiful and ancient building for worship at the Reformation in 1536, may have been modified by the persistence of a Catholic tradition at the Priory until at least 1564, when a candle burned in honour of St Nicholas in the Priory Church (Figure 3) in defiance of official Church of England rules. This suggests a toleration and sympathy for the Roman religion by non-Catholics who were possible church papists. There is a strong probability that when the time came, the attic of a house in Church Street, later used by the Jacobites to accommodate Bonnie Prince Charlie in 1745, was used as a Mass Centre occasionally. The origins of the Leonardgate/Mason Street Mass Centre and the erection of St Peter's, Dalton Square Chapel, have been mentioned above (Figure 4). The congregation of the latter were vigorous and enterprising and urgently sought a graveyard and adequate school facilities for their children, for the tiny school in Friars passage was inadequate. Attempts to put land south of the town near the Pointer at Greaves fell through, and the secretary of the Catholic School Board, wealthy Thomas Coulston, decided the only way to ensure progress lay with entrusting the project to the Clergy. On 7 September 1849, a group of entrepreneurs including Thomas's uncle Gabriel Coulston, John Whiteside and Richard Jenkinson, negotiated the sale of land priced at £2,150

> *between Moor Lane and the canal bridge in the fryarage, also land called green or greenfield close bounded in the south by a road leading to certain stone quarries and by the new* [East] *road lately put in by the vendor, known as long meadow;*

from the vendor, Henry Gregson, on the Greenfield site where St Peter's Cathedral now stands. An indenture of Mortgage of the 14 February, 1850, was made to the 'R[ight] Rev[erend] George Brown DD, the Very Rev[erend] H Gradwell, the Rev[erend] Joseph Walmsley'. The schedule is signed by Richard Brown, James Whiteside and Thomas Coulston, and dated 15 August 1855. Thus, the land was transferred into the ownership of the church before the building of St Peter's began, but after the opening of the cemetery,

Figure 4. St Peter's Cathedral, Lancaster. *Author's collection*

schools and convent. The cemetery was opened in 1850, the schools in 1851 and St Walburge's Convent, which housed the teachers, in 1853. In 1856, Thomas Coulston bequested £2,000 for the building of a new church, augmented by the promise of £1,000 from Miss Anne Coulston, daughter of Gabriel mentioned above, and the death of John Whiteside later in the year resulted in a donation of £3,000 from his brother James. Miss Dalton of Thurnham also promised £1,000 for the building and endowment of a Lady Chapel. Several rows of houses envisaged on the original plan were never built, thus depriving the project of essential funds for the maintenance of the building. Richard Melchides Brown (1802-68) is credited with the considerable success of building the Church. The foundation stone was blessed by Dr Alexander Goss, Bishop of Liverpool, on April 29 1858. The new St Peter's Church and presbytery were completed to the design of Edward Graham Paley of Lancaster and Edmund Sharpe in 1859, although shortage of funds caused some changes to the design, and some of the decoration was not completed until the church was re-ordered in 1998. The firms of Austin and Paley, successor to Paley and Sharpe, have done much further work on the complex of buildings.[9]

The vision of Protestant and Catholic churches working in harmony would have been unthinkable to many recusant Catholic and Protestants of the past. Perhaps the irony is that both St Peter's Catholic and St Mary's Church of England churches, are now substantially supported by the nation as works of historic interest and architecture. Only a few Christians, a minority of the general population, like the tiny Protestant and Catholic recusant congregations of the seventeenth century, see the church as a spiritual resource, vital to the moral welfare of the nation. Perhaps, things are not really so different in this second Millennium since the birth of the man who began it all.

Notes and References

1. Potter, T W and Andrews, R D, 'Excavation at St Patrick's Chapel and St. Peter's Church, Heysham, Lancashire, 1977-8', *Contrebis*, XXI (1996), pp.29-73; Bagley, *A History of Lancashire*, (Henley, 1970), pp.12-23; Noble, A J (ed), Henry Taylor, *The Ancient Crosses and Wells of Lancashire*, Vol. 1 Lonsdale Hundred, (Wigan, 1999).

2. Anon, *Visitor's Guide*, St Michael & All Angels Church, Beetham (undated); White, A, 'Some Notes of Medieval Hornby, *Contrebis*, XXII (Lancaster, 1986), pp.1-5; Bagley, *A History of Lancashire*, (Henley, 1970), pp.16-17; White, A, 'Setting the Scene, 1193-1500', White, A (ed), *A History of Lancaster 1193-1993*, (Keele, 1993) pp.31-41 [hereafter HoL]; White, A, *Lancaster a Pictorial History*, (Chichester, 1990) fig.5; Billington, R N & Brownbill, J, *St Peter's Lancaster* (London, 1910), pp.3-13 [hereafter B&B]; Anon, *History of Lancaster Priory and Parish Church*,

(Lancaster, c1944), p.15, 16; Mullett, M, *Reformation and Renewal*, in White, A (ed), HoL, p.55.

3. B&B, pp.13-75; Mullett, M, *Reformation and Renewal*, in White, A (ed), HoL, p 59; Hilton, J A, 'The Cisalpines' in Hilton, J A (ed), *A Catholic of the Enlightenment Essays of Lingard's Work and Times*, (Wigan, 1999), p 12; Lambert, S *Monks, Martyrs and Mayors*, (Lancaster, 1995), folio 9 recto; B&B, pp.84-89; White, Andrew, 'Gentlemen's Houses in Lancaster', *Georgian Group Journal*, VI, (1996) pp.120-130; Anon, *History of Lancaster Priory and Parish Church*, (Lancaster, c1944), p.18.

4. Gardner, N (ed), *Lancashire Recusants*, 1678, 1679, 1682, 3 Vols., (Wigan, 1998, 1999,) [hereafter LR]; Walsham, *A Church Papists*, (Woodbridge, 1999) [hereafter ChP], pp.111-115.

5. Gardner, N, LR, 1682, passim, LR 1679, pp 6-7; Dalziel, N, 'Trade and Transition: 1690-1815', White, A (ed), HoL, p 107; B&B, pp 55-65; Hilton, J A, 'The Catholic revival in Thurnham 1785-1848', *North West Catholic History*, XII, (Wigan, 1985), pp 1-5, [hereafter NWCH]; Hudson, P, 'The Lost Treasure of Dolphinlee', *Contrebis*, Vol. XXIV, 1999, pp 21-21; Hilton, J A et al, *Bishop Leyburn's Confirmation Register* of 1687, (Wigan, 1997); Walsham, A ChP, p 118; Foley, B C, *Some People of Penal Times*, (Lancaster, 1991) [hereafter SOPPT]; Anstruther, G, *The Seminary Priests*, 1716-1800, Vol. 4, (4 Vols., Great Wakering, 1968-1977), p.24.

6. Foley, B C, Mss Lancaster Paper c.1798 (unpublished); Anstruther, G, ibid.; Foley, B C, SPPT, pp 25-37; Lambert, S, *Monks, Martyrs and Mayors*, (Lancaster, 1991), Fol. 8, verso 9; B&B, pp 83-99.

7. Dalziel, N, *Trade and Transition, 1690-1815*, White, A (ed), HoL, pp. 91-144; Noble, A J, 'Lancaster Catholics Towards Emancipation', NWCH, XXV (1998); Foley, B C, SOPPPT, pp.113-122; Gardner, N, ' Coulstons of Lunesdale and Lancaster' [hereafter CLL], NWCH, XXV (1998); Hilton, J A (ed) *A Catholic Enlightenment* (Wigan, 1999); Hilton, J A, 'The Catholic Revival in Thurnham, 1785-1848', NWCH, XII, (1985), pp 1-2; Bamber, J 'Yealand Bi-Centenary and Restoration of the Chapel', NWCH, X, (1983), p 34; *Lancaster Diocesan Directory* 1997 (Preston, 1996), pp.26-55.

8. Gardner, N & Baird, R, 'Genealogy' (unpublished), p.1; Winstanley, M 'The Town Transformed 1815-1914', White, A (ed), HoL, pp 145-198; Price, J W A, *The Industrial Archaeology of the Lune Valley*, CNWRS Occasional Papers, 12 (Lancaster, 1983); Winstanley, M, 'The Town Transformed: 1815-1914', White, A (ed), HoL, pp.147-149.

9. Mullett, M, *Reformation and Renewal, 1450-1690*, White, A (ed) Hol, p 60; Gardner, N, 'CLL', NWCH, XXV, (1998); Lancs Record Office, Preston, RCLn 2/21,RCLn 9/68; Lambert, S, *Monks Martyrs and Mayors,* Fols. 9, 10; B&B, pp.103-105.

3. THE QUAY TO SUCCESS: DEVELOPING AN EIGHTEENTH CENTURY PORT

by Peter Williamson

IN 1750 CONSTRUCTION WORK BEGAN on the imposing riverside development of St George's Quay, much of which is still in evidence today. During the seventeenth and eighteenth centuries Britain witnessed a commercial revolution which led to the transformation of small coastal market centres into important international ports. Merchant adventurers were at the forefront in expanding the British Empire across the world, and domestic port facilities had to be developed to cater for this increased demand. Borough Corporations often instigated this process, and, in Lancaster, it was achieved through the newly created Port Commission of 1750. Without the quay, the port many not have developed to the extent it did, and Lancaster may never have experienced the so-called 'Golden Age', between c1770 and c1800.

As Sharpe points out 'English trade in 1550 was essentially limited to the North Sea and Atlantic coast of Europe, but by 1760 it was global in its extent'.[1] Langford agrees that 'this switch from European to colonial markets can be discerned before the 1720s, but as a development of unmistakable importance it belongs to the mid-eighteenth century'.[2] Nowhere was this more true than in Lancaster.

A Question of Speculation

In 1747 'an Act for improving the navigation of the river *Loyne*, otherwise called *Lune*, and for building a quay or wharf near the town of *Lancaster*', was drawn up by the Borough Corporation and merchant community. To the great satisfaction of all, it was passed two years later, by Pelham's ministry, on 16 November 1749 (Figure 1).

In Liverpool, port facilities had been developed from as early as 1700, but without the need for a specific Port Commission. This suggests that Lancaster was not only slow in responding to opportunities, but also that, Lancaster Corporation played a far more limited role in stimulating trade, than that in Liverpool. Ashton agrees that 'the initiative in Liverpool came from the Corporation [leading members of which were ship-owners and merchants]'.[3] In Hull work was carried out by 'a company consisting of the

Anno Regni
GEORGII II.

R E G I S
Magnæ Britanniæ, Franciæ, & Hiberniæ,
V I C E S I M O   T E R T I O.

At the Parliament begun and holden at *Weſtminſter,* the Tenth Day of *November, Anno Dom.* 1747, in the Twenty firſt Year of the Reign of our Sovereign Lord *GEORGE* the Second, by the Grace of God, of *Great Britain, France,* and *Ireland,* King, Defender of the Faith, *&c.*

And from thence continued by ſeveral Prorogations to the Sixteenth Day of *November,* 1749, being the Third Seſſion of this preſent Parliament.

L O N D O N:
Printed by *Thomas Baſkett,* Printer to the King's moſt Excellent Majeſty; and by the Aſſigns of *Robert Baſkett.* 1749.

Figure 1. Copy of the Act of 1749.

Corporation, the brotherhood of shipmasters and several individuals',[4] whilst in Lancaster it was the Port Commission, albeit backed by the Corporation.

Several Port Commissions were set up around the country at this time, but Lancaster was one of only four in which 'the electors [were] ship-owners and merchants as payers of dock dues.'[5] In essence three things were needed – the right to levy tolls on all shipping loading or unloading in the port; the right to build a quay and associated warehouses; and the right to improve the navigation of the river by means of dredging and buoys. It would appear that, although the constitutional history of any port is quite complex, in the end it boiled down to money. The prime responsibility of a port authority was to be credit worthy so that it could borrow money to pay for whatever works it proposed. This is exactly what the Port Commission in Lancaster was established for.

Quaker Seclusion

Initial comparisons, between Corporation and Commission Minute Books, immediately illustrate that there appears to be a little difference in the personnel in authority on both bodies. It, therefore, begs the question why was there a specific Port Commission in Lancaster? One possible explanation surrounds the involvement of the local Quaker community. Many were wealthy merchants who had entered trade, manufacture and business, and, through astute business acumen and hard work, had built a nation-wide network of 'Friends' with tremendous financial influence. They were, therefore, not to be overlooked lightly.

However, their refusal to take the oath of allegiance or the sacrament of the Anglican Church saw them barred from holding any civic office. With much money to invest and much mercantile influence in the town, it may have been imperative for the Corporation to find a way of including these men in the affairs of the port. Only by setting up a separate body could this be done, and hence the creation of the Port Commission in 1750.

However, this was not the only reason. Such an independent body had two other important advantages for both the Corporation and the Commission. Firstly, any financial losses would be the Commissioners' losses and not the Corporation's; and secondly, all income could be directed towards improvements of port facilities, rather than being put to other uses by the Corporation.

The merchants of Lancaster, therefore, duly raised the necessary money for the Act and it was passed. They now had the authority to form a Port Commission and the means 'to raise Money... for the Term of Twenty one Years... for every Ship, Vessel, or Lighter, coming into or going out of the said Port of *Lancaster*'.[6] In other words they were to be a credit worthy organisation with the ability to raise money using the promise of incoming revenues as collateral for such borrowing.

Corporation Support

The first Commissioners were elected for five years, being '*Merchants* possessed of a Sixteenth, or other greater Share of any Ship of Fifty Tons of upwards, actually belonging to the Port of *Lancaster*',[7] and then every three years thereafter. In other words, the Act specifically gave control of the port to a Commission of ship-owning merchantmen, rather than simply leaving future development in the hands of the Corporation, who would not necessarily have its best interests at heart. However, as Dalziel points out, in reality this actually meant that 'the mayor and many members of the Corporation were able to pursue the borough's interest as elected Commissioners'.[8] It would appear that the Corporation supported the Commission, just as the Commission, in turn, supported the Borough.

In 1750 the very first appointees were Frances Reynolds, the Mayor of Lancaster, with Edward Marton,[9] Allan Harrison, Dr James Fenton, Oliver Marton, George Gibson and Miles Barber. These 'substantial' men were joined by the merchants 'William Butterfield, Myles Birket, William Gillison, Abraham Rawlinson, Robert Foxcroft, Robert Lawson, the younger Henry Williamson, Henry White, John Bowes and Thomas Satterthwaite'.[10] More than half of the original Commission appointed, therefore, were international merchants, and of those, Birket, Satterthwaite, Lawson, and Rawlinson, were Quakers.

The Butterfield family had long associations with the area and were heavily involved in the African slave trade, an integral part in the cycle of production, manufacture and sale. Sugar was one prime example of a new taste which caught on in Europe, was harvested by slaves, and which prompted the Quaker Lawsons of Lancaster to build a sugarhouse in the town. As Schofield argues, 'merchants and ship's captains dealing with colonial markets could appreciate the demands for slaves, when so many colonial products depended on slave labour'.[11] Unfortunately, they were not the only merchants to do so.

Cotton and Slaves

From as early as the 1730s, the Quaker Miles Birket was trading with Barbados, and when his daughter, Elizabeth, married Dodshon Foster (Figure 2) in 1753, the involvement increased. It is somewhat

Figure 2. Portrait if Dodshon Foster, by William Tate, c.1780. *Courtesy of Lancaster City Museum*

surprising that Quakers became involved in the slave trade, but at that time, no qualms about this seemed to have existed. Foster's partner, another Quaker, John Heathcote, married the sister of Thomas Satterthwaite, and together, they traded with Africa and the West Indies in their ship *Barlborough*, built in Lancaster and fitted out for the slave trade. Both Foster and Heathcote went on to be elected Port Commissioners in 1755.

The Satterthwaites were another Quaker family that dealt in slaves. Benjamin acted as factor in Barbados for the Townson-Dilworth-Rawlinson group between 1734 and 1741.[12] In many similar cases, merchant families like these operated together, spreading risks among several firms. Benjamin Satterthwaite was the stepson of Miles Towson and the nephew of John Dilworth. Meanwhile, Benjamin's brother, Thomas, had gone into a partnership with Charles Inman, ex-apprentice of the Butterfields, and by 1753, they too, were recorded as slave traders.

The Rawlinsons, too, decided to send a son, Abraham II, to Barbados in 1736 to learn first-hand experience of the West Indies trade.[13] Another son, Thomas, also entered the colonial trade, having married Mary Dilworth in 1734, whose father was already linked to the family through trade. The Rawlinsons went on to dominate the West Indies trade in Lancaster through links with Thomas Touchet,[14] a cotton trader from Manchester. They exported Lancashire's manufactured cotton goods to the colonies, while importing raw cotton to England. Of their connection with the slave trade there can be little doubt, for in 1752, it was also recorded that they had '20 new negroes aboard the *Providence*'.[15]

Ambrose Gillison was in partnership with John Bowes, and captained their ship, the *Ann*, to the Americas. Gillison was eventually succeeded by his son William, duly appointed Port Commissioner in 1750, whilst both were known to have trading partnerships with other families, like the Butterfields.

The Quaker Lawsons also had long business links with Lancaster, and in particular those relating to sea-borne trade. In 1720 Robert Lawson had built a quay and warehouses at Sunderland Point,[16] and sent at least five vessels to Barbados before 1738.[17] Like the Rawlinsons, the Lawson family, too, had the advantage of close ties with another Manchester Quaker cotton merchant, Isaac Moss.[18]

Competition or Shared Interest?
When the Port Commission first met in April, 1750, the afore-mentioned merchants were among the key figures in its

administration. Similarly, on the Corporation, it was virtually the same local *men of substance* who controlled the Council. Council electors were held on 28 October, 1750, when Thomas Postlethwaite was elected mayor,[19] and on the Council were Nicholas Atkinson, James Thompson, Henry Williamson, John Bowes, Henry White, Robert Foxcroft, Abraham Rawlinson, William Gillison, and Henry Hargreaves - all Port Commissioners at some time during the early-1750s. In fact, six of them were simultaneously on the Port Commission.[20]

One typical example of this shared interest came when representatives of the Council met on 2 March, 1757, at the Merchants' Coffee House in Lancaster, 'to consult with an equal number of Port Commissioners',[21] regarding the building of soughs[22] and bridges along Lancaster Marsh. The Port Commission elected Thomas Hutton Rawlinson (Figure 3), Charles Inman, Nicholas

Figure 3. Portrait of Thomas Hutton Rawlinson (1712-69), by George Romney. *Courtesy of Lancaster City Museum*

Atkinson, James Barrow and John Helme for that purpose, and yet, Barrow, Atkinson and Inman were on the Council. The Corporation meanwhile, chose Miles Barber, Joshua Bryer, Henry Williamson, Henry Hargreaves and George Gray, three of whom were also Port Commissioners. Bryer's daughter was married to Port Trustee Thomas Hinds (elected 1755), and George Gray was employed by the Commission on the building of the quay wall.

The close-knit community of Lancaster merchants was intertwined at every level, through business links and family ties and marriage. Lancaster was an important port in the eighteenth century, but it was also very small, and so contact between the trading elements in the town would have been very difficult to avoid. The advantage now was that, through this Commission, the town also had the benefit and experience of the very influential Quaker merchant community.

Quarrying the Stone

At the first meeting of the Commissioners, on 30 April 1750, twenty-three plans were drawn up for the building of the quay and the tenders were invited for the work. The idea was quite simple – to build a wall at the river's edge, and then to infill the space behind and level off the top, thereby creating an area where warehouses could be built. Finding enough stone locally was not a problem, as there were some thirty-eight quarries on nearby Windmill Hill.[24]

On 17 May 1750, the task of building *phase one* of the quay wall was given to the Quaker William Kirkby & Co, Masons, at 9s 9d [48p] per yard, twenty-five to run from the 'weigh-house to the *Summer Pasture*'. It was

> to be nine feet at the foundations and then to be a breadth of 8 feet and upwards in front and backwards to diminish to 3 feet at the top, in good workman-like manner - the stones to be from Windmill Hill and no other place.[26]

There is no mention of how or when the quay became named after St George, although the name appears on all the original plans and maps. At this time the second of the Hanoverian kings was on the throne, and it would appear to have been the patriotic thing to do, particularly in view of recent Jacobite revivals.

The original *Act* of 1749 not only governed the building of the quay, but also authorised improvement of the navigation of shipping. These 'improvements to the navigation' generally took three forms: the removal of obstructions from the river-bed or banks; the positioning of strategic buoys at the mouth of the river and on dangerous sandbars; and the building of a road down the quay and across the Marsh, from which the progress of ships to and from the port could be tracked.

Capital Security

However, those who invested in the Act of Parliament in the first place now wished to see some return for their money. Abraham Rawlinson and Myles Birket had invested £500 to initiate the process, and on 30 October 1750, it was agreed to 'grant them duties sop obtained under the Act as security'. However, more money was still needed as new investors still sought. One influential supporter of the scheme was Miss Ellen Butterfield, whose brother William was a Port Commissioner. In all, she invested over £1000 and recouped her investment through dividends and repayments taken from the incoming duties. Such capital investment allowed the quay to continue apace, so much so, that on 9 October, 1751, the sale of the first thirty-five 'lotts' by auction took place.

The land created on the new quay wall allowed for a major development programme in the banks of the river Lune in Lancaster. Streets were laid out, and their names duly recorded on the plan. King, Queen, Prince's and Duke Streets were joined by Marton Street, Loyne Street and Custom House Alley, which ran parallel to the quay. An annual rent of four shillings [20p] was payable on those properties overlooking the river, whilst those at the back were rated at three shillings [15p] per year.

Bidding was brisk and twenty-six bids were placed between nine interested parties for the very first 'lott' to be auctioned, Thomas Gibson eventually taking it for sixteen pounds. The remaining 'lotts' went to Robert Baldwin, Henry White (with Myles Birket), William Dilworth, Thomas and William Satterthwiate, Abraham Rawlinson and Joisah Whalley. Several of these bought more than one 'lott;, preferably adjoining, for more substantial developments. It is possible that merchants such as Dilworth wanted high prestige front 'lotts' to illuminate their standing in the community, whilst also buying less significant 'lotts' at the back for more mundane purposes. Over fifty per cent of the purchasers were serving Port Commissioners.

Construction Site

Most of the new warehouses that came to be built along the quay, were a distinctive type of three or four-storeyed buildings. Large loading doors on each floor are flanked by windows, and at the top wooden, later metal, cranes were installed to hoist goods up to the upper floors. Two of these are still in place today. As White points out, 'little control was exercised over what was built and mixture of private houses, inns and warehouses of varying character resulted'.[29]

By 9 April 1752, the Commissioners had agreed to extend the wall a further seventy yards down the river, and

> *that Henry White, John Bowes, Robert Foxcroft and George Gray place adverts out for workmen to present their proposals.*[28]

The construction was exactly the same as before, with Thomas Walker winning the contract at '10s 8d [53p] per yard, superficial measure in the ffront, and agreeable to the proposals of the purpose'.[29]

By 31 May 1753, it was resolved that the quay area already staked out around the sold 'lotts' should be paved, and a further six months later the second auction took place.[30] On Wednesday, 7 November 1753, at the *White Hart*, seven new 'lotts' were sold, although 'lotts' thirty-six to thirty-eight were withdrawn and earmarked for the erection of a Custom House. The port had outgrown the current Custom House, and Port Commission were looking to make a statement about themselves and their town by erecting a Custom House that would demonstrate to any visitor that Lancaster was a port of great significance and importance.

Coffee and Ships

The newly built warehouses allowed for the speedy and efficient storage of produce straight from the ships' holds.[31] Not that all were erected immediately. Mackreth's map of 1778 (Figure 4) shows that

Figure 4. Mackreth's map of 1778, showing the quay development. *Courtesy of Lancaster Reference Library*

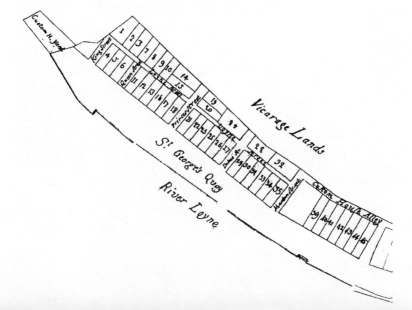

although John Nicholson had built on his 'lotts' purchased in 1753, those bought by William Gillison at the same time were standing empty. However, ships sailing into the newly developed port by 1755 would still have been met by a 'state-of-the-art' architectural storage facilities, certainly in terms of this particular port.

All the activity in this newly-developed port was governed by strict bye-laws, which dictated rules for tying up at the quayside: ships had to be unloaded as quickly as possible; homeward bound ships were allowed 'to have an inside berth at one of the slips in preference to ships taking on board their outward cargo',[32] and 'no carter shall presume to drive over any of the ships' cable or ends made fast to the quay rings on forfeiture of one shilling for very such offence'.[33] Five hundred copies were printed for distribution to 'the Captains as they arrive and each Captain in the port to have one'.[34] Meanwhile, a post was fixed opposite the Summer Pasture for the shipping and re-shipping of gunpowder.[35]

On 20 November 1755, it was agreed, at a meeting at the Merchants' Coffee House, to once again extend the quay wall. The Coffee House had become an important meeting place for merchants and their business partners and many transactions took place there. In Lancaster a Coffee House was established in Market Street (Figure 5), and here ships' brokers did the deals that allowed ships' captain to

Figure 5. The Merchants' Coffee House (with bay windows) in Market Street, Lancaster. *Courtesy of Lancaster City Museum*

stay at sea, whilst they made preparations for future voyages.

Customs and Specifications

The money raised through investment and duties allowed for a perch, 'with lanthorn on top' at abbey Scar at the mouth of the Lune, but more importantly, for the new Custom House. The third successful auction of 'lotts' had taken place on 16 December 1756, and the Atlantic trade had created a considerable increase in

Figure 6. Richard Gillow's Palladian-style Custom House of 1763. *Courtesy of Lancaster City Museum*

disposable wealth in Lancaster. As White points out 'from about 1750 to 1820 this wealth was at a peak and expressed itself in fine new buildings both public and private'.[36] Many had been built in the town, and the quay was not to be deprived of its crowning glory. Work began, to Richard Gillow's design, in 1763, on the afore-mentioned three vacant 'lotts' from phase two. The contractor was Richard Fisher, who, in 1755, had built the third phase of the quay wall, with Robert Clarkson agreeing to 'perform the slating and plasterers work'.[37] The specification provided that the columns were to be of one piece of stone each, and to be fashioned from Mainstone Quarry in Ellel.[38] Gillow was a member of the Lancaster cabinet-making family and his Palladian design (Figure 6) 'reflected the port's new-found assurance and economic prospecrity'.[39]

One final auction of 'lotts' took place on 21 February 1781, and this saw the last major development on the quay. The original aims and objectives of the Commissioners seem to have been met: the river was easier to navigate and St George's Quay now provided ships with modern facilities for loading, unloading and storage. Evolutionary processes may have made Liverpool the port it was, but a small revolution in the early 1750s helped Lancaster enjoy its so-called 'Golden Age' over the next thirty years (Figure 7).

Figure 7. St George's Quay (no date). *Courtesy of Lancaster City Museum*

A Qualified Success

The Port Commission of 1750 had given the mercantile men of Lancaster the authority an opportunity to develop their port and build a quay with modern facilities. What is important to understand is that many influential merchants, though the Corporation, were driven to take such action by the growing opportunities in international trade throughout the world. The completion of the quay heralded in an age of unprecedented prosperity, and this is very much in evidence today in the number if grand buildings erected during the Georgian period, and especially along the quay.

The increase in world trade was the key to Britain's success as a maritime, mercantile nation in the eighteenth century, but the key which heralded in Lancaster's most successful economic era, was built of stone.

Primary Sources

The Port Commission Records are held by Lancaster Reference Library and Lancaster City and Maritime Museums.
All record are available on request via the relevant body or Museum. The Borough Corporation Records are held by Lancaster City Museum.

Notes and References

1. Sharpe, J A, *Early Modern England - a social history 1550-1760* (London 1993), p.136.
2. Langford, P, *A Polite and Commercial People, England 1727-1783.* (Oxford, 1993), p.168.
3. Ashton, T S, *An Economic History of England: the 18th Century* (London 1972), p.142.
4. *ibid.*, p.142.
5. Webb, S & B, *English Local Government: Statutory Authorities for Special Purposes* (London, 1922), p.266.
6. *An Act to Improve the Navigation of the River Loyne,* (1749), p.267.
7. *ibid.*, p.266.
8. White, A (ed), *A History of Lancaster 1193-1993* (Keele, 1993), p.104.
9. Edward Marton was also MP of Lancaster from 1747 until his death in 1758.
10. An Act ..., p.266.
11. Schofield, M M, 'The Slave Trade from Lancashire and Cheshire Ports outside Liverpool', c1750-1790, in *Transactions of the Historic Society of Lancsahire and Cheshire* (1976) Vol. 126, p.36.
12. Schofield, M M, *The Letter Book of Benjamin Satterthwaite of Lancaster,* 1737-1744 (1960), p.129.
13. *ibid.*, p.24.
14. Elder, M, *The Slave Trade and the Economic Development of 18th Century Lancaster,* 1737-1744 (Halifax, 1992), p.26.
15. The Will of Thomas Hutton Rawlinson, 1766, Lancaster Maritime Museum.
16. Elder, The Slave Trade, p.24.
17. *ibid.*, p.24.
18. *ibid.*, p.24.
19. Corporation of Lancaster Complaints and Elections, 1736-1756 (E), 1st November, 1750.
20. Namely, Henry Williamson, John Bowes, Henry White, Robert Foxcroft, Abraham Rawlinson, and William Gillison.

21. Complaints and Elections, 1736-1756, (E), 12 January, 1757.
22. 'Sough' - also called an adit, a passage like vault, cut out from under the earth to drain water.
23. Port Commission Minutes, 30 April, 1750.
24. 'Windmill Hill' is now crowned with Ashton Memorial, and the quarries are still visible within Williamson Park, which was landscaped at the end of the nineteenth century.
25. Port Commission Minutes, 7 May, 1750, at Sergeant Padgett's.
26. *ibid.*, 29 April, 1752, at the *Nags Head.*
27. White, A, *The Buildings of Georgian Lancaster,* (Lancaster, 1992), p.21.
28. Port Commission Minutes, 9 April, 1752, at the *Golden Anchor.*
29. *ibid.*, 29 April, 1752, at the *Nags Head.*
30. *ibid.*, 31 May, 1753.
31. Many of these are still standing today, converted into flats, and are listed buildings.
32. Port Commission Minutes, 5th December, 1753.
33. *ibid.*, 5 December, 1753.
34. *ibid.*, 3 July, 1755, at the *Three Tuns on the Quay.*
35. Near where Powder House Lane runs today.
36. White, A, 'Stone Masons on a Georgian Town', in *Local Historian*, 21, no. 2 (1991) p60.
37. Proposals for Building a new Custom House upon St George's Quay, 17 December, 1762.
38. *ibid.*
39. Dalziel, N, *Lancaster Maritime Museum*, (Lancaster, 1992).

4. THE RISE AND FALL OF THE STAINED GLASS TRADE IN NINETEENTH CENTURY LANCASTER

by Suzanne Boutin

AT THE BEGINNING OF the nineteenth century there were only a handful of practising stained glass craftsmen up and down the country. A large amount of windows were produced in London, or by workshops in large provincial cities and towns such as Birmingham, Liverpool, Newcastle and Bristol. There were also a considerable number of middle-sized firms in towns such as Manchester, Shrewsbury, Lancaster, Leeds, York, Newcastle, Edinburgh and Glasgow, which were established by the mid-nineteenth century.[1]

Lancaster stained glass had its beginnings as early as 1825, when Charles Seward began making stained glass in the Old Music Room in Sun Street (Figure 1). A stained glass East window made by Mr

Figure 1. The Old Music Room, Sun Street, Lancaster. Once used by Sewards for their stained glass work. *Author's collection*

Seward of Lancaster, in St Peter's church, Fylde Road, Preston, was mentioned in an 1825 trade directory.[2] The firm was also responsible in making the stained glass windows for St Anne's Church, Lancaster. In 1778, Charles Seward, brazier and tin plate worker, had established his firm in Lancaster. He eventually held a Royal appointment, granted by George III.[3] Sewards also held a contract for the Lancaster Corporation in the early days of the eighteenth century, for lighting the town with oil lamps, prior to the introduction of gas.[4]

Charles's second son, also called Charles, married Miss Mary Shrigley, whose family were well-known painters and gilders in Lancaster. Charles Seward died in 1930.[5] The firm continued until the 1970s.

A Seward and Company, and later Shrigley and Hunt, had the monopoly of the stain glass trade in Lancaster for about sixteen years until a third stained glass firm, Easton and Bulfield, opened their

Figure 2. Thomas a Beckett Window, the Priory Church, Lancaster. Made by Abbott and Company Ltd. *Author's collection*

studio in King Street in 1886. Both men had previously worked for the firm of Shrigley and Hunt.

The only firm in Lancaster to rival that of Shrigley and Hunt for its stained glass work was William Abbott, who originally commenced in business in the town as a plumber and glazier in 1860. It was at the turn of the century that stained glass was introduced into the business. The firm became well known, both in this country and aboard, for their craftwork. Like Shrigley and Hunt, Abbots also carried out stained glass commissions for all religious denominations (Figure 2).

After the retirement of Mr J E H Abbott, grandson of the founder, the firm's business at St John's Studio in Chapel Street, Lancaster, which was later owned by Cosalt Limited of Grimsby and managed by Mr George Reay, closed (Figure 3).

Figure 3. Abbott and Co Ltd Offices, Chapel Street, Lancaster. *Author's collection*

Reference to the trade directories from 1879-1938 shows that there were nine firms making stained glass in the town at various times. Out of these nine firms, only three firms practised the craft for a considerable length of time. These were Shrigley and Hunt, A Seward and Company and Abbott and Company. Some of the other Lancaster Studios concentrated more on assembling leaded windows rather than creating stained glass, and some of these firms only practised the craft for relatively short periods of time. Today, 2001, there are two stained glass firms working in the area, and a few in Cumbria.

ABBOTT AND COMPANY St John's Studio, Lancaster	
Lancaster	St Mary's, Priory Church
Morecambe	St Christopher's Church The Church of the Ascension Emmanuel Church
Fleetwood	Rossall School
Preston	The Royal Infirmary
Great Harwood	St John's Church
Burnley	St Peter's Church
Chorley	Brindle Church
Haslingden	St John's Church
Clitheroe	Trinity Central Methodist Church

Table 1: Showing some of the Churches and Buildings where the Stained Glass work of Abbott and Company can be seen.

The firm of Shrigley and Hunt started in the 1770s, when a craftsman known as 'Shrigley of London' started business as a painter in the town.[6] In 1795, Thomas Shrigley died in Preston. The business in Lancaster then passed to his son, Thomas, who was listed in a trade directory of 1799 as a painter and oilman of New Road, Lancaster.[7]

The premises later moved to 148, Church Street which was at the corner of Church Street and China Lane, Lancaster. When Thomas had died in 1821, the business passed to his son, Joseph, who died in 1836. It was after Joseph's death that his widow, Ellen, took James

Williamson into partnership.[8] James Williamson, later to become the father of Lord Ashton, lodged above Shrigley's workshops during his working life.[9] It was at this time, with the introduction of picture framing, that the firm also began to specialise in mural paintings, some of which can be seen in the apse of St John's church in Lancaster. These included the *Decalogue* (the Ten Commandment) panels, painted by James Williamson. The firm continued trading as Shrigley and Williamson for about seven years, when the partnership was dissolved. In 1857, the firm of Shrigley had their estimate accepted in painting, staining and varnishing the new Catholic church of St Peter's, which was built on East Road, Lancaster. The church was completed by 1859.[10] After Ellen Shrigley died, her son Joseph continued to run the business until he died in 1869[11] at the age of forty-five years, leaving a widow, Eliza, and a family of eight children to bring up.[12] This was a crucial time for the widow who was left with a business to run and a large family. The firm continued for two years under the name of Hudson, Shrigley and Company, as Eliza Shrigley's maiden name had been Hunt.

In 1870, Arthur William Hunt (1848-1917), a designer and decorator from Hoddesden near London[13] took over control of the firm from Mrs Shrigley. It was also about this time, that the firm became known as Shrigley and Hunt. It was in 1873, after Eliza Shrigley had died, and A W Hunt became the owner, that the firm moved to new premises at 16 Castle Hill, Lancaster. A W Hunt was responsible for the introduction of the stained glass trade into the business. During the early years, the firm tended to concentrate on the church and house decorating side of the business, as well as the tile painting and stained glass work.

The firm received many commissions for decorating some of the large houses and estates situated in and around Lancaster during this period. These included, The Greaves, Lancaster, for E Paley Esq, Ellel Grange for E Preston Esq, and Quernmore Park for Q Garnett Esq.[14] The tile painting was introduced into the firm with the arrival of A W Hunt. Decorative tile work was popular both for churches and homes during the nineteenth century. Shrigley and Hunt engaged Mr W Lambert, a tile-painting expert from the Potteries, to carry out this work. It was not unusual for firms such as Shrigley and Hunt to make both decorative materials and stained glass. The firms of James Powell of Whitefriars Studios, London, and the Charles E Kempe Studios also made decorative materials as well as stained glass.[15]

The stained glass branch of the Shrigley and Hunt firm developed from about 1876, this was during a period when church architecture had been experiencing the effects of the Gothic Revival which included the building of new churches and also the restoration of many older ones in the Gothic style. This had a profound effect upon the stained glass trade.[16]

Lancaster's location made it possible to develop a market in areas further north, such as in Cumberland, Westmorland, Northumberland, and also into Scotland and across to Ireland.

Four stained glass experts were engaged by Shrigley and Hunt to design and make stained glass windows. These included Carl Almquist, a Swede who was also a member of the Henry Holiday Circle of Stained Glass Artists, in London. Henry Holiday was one of the leading glass artists and designers of the Victorian period. Carl Almquist was employed as chief designer for the firm, and the other three craftsmen, E H Jewitt, A Berridge and W Eames, each served the firm for half a century.[17]

These craftsmen introduced a revival of the genuine craft of stained glass that had been overshadowed for a number of years by painted glass produced by a technique of applying enamels to clear glass through the means of a brush. It is generally agreed that artistically such windows were far the inferior of genuine stained glass, and they were certainly much less translucent, often being muddy in overall tone.

It was when the tile painting began to decline due to reproduction of cheap tiles being manufactured in the Potteries, that Shrigley and Hunt began concentrating entirely on ecclesiastical stained glass and church decorative work that include reredoses, murals, frescos, and brasses.

'The Studio' became renowned for their beautiful stained glass windows nor only in Lancaster but in other parts of the country and also abroad. Their work included memorial and heraldic windows, as well as windows for many churches and important buildings (Figure 4)[19] and decorative stained glass work for shipping companies.

The firm made over 50 stained glass windows in churches and chapels in Lancaster, and over 500 in Lancashire, and 5,000 windows in Great Britain, Ireland and other parts of the world.

Shrigley and Hunt also made stained glass windows for Paley and Austin, the well known Lancaster architects, who were responsible for designing and building several churches and important buildings and estates in and around Lancaster, as well as other parts of Lancashire.

Figure 4. The Memorial Window, the Priory Church, Lancaster. Made by Shrigley and Hunt. *Author's collection*

Another important feature of Shrigley and Hunt's work was their domestic glass, used in door panels, screens, bedroom and staircase windows in many middle class residences during this period.

Although A W Hunt was a devoted churchman, and a member of the Priory Church in Lancaster, where, for some time he was Vicar's warden, he readily accepted commissions for church windows for all religious denominations both in Lancaster and other parts of the country. The firm made windows for several Catholic churches, including St Peter's, Lancaster, where they installed a memorial window to Mary Smith at a cost of £300.[20] Shrigley and Hunt also gave a stained glass clerestory window representing a seraphim to St Peter's church in 1904.

As the stained glass trade increased, Shrigley and Hunt began employing more staff. During the 1880s, the firm was employing about fifteen to twenty men, including apprentices who served up to a seven-year indentureship in the trade.

SHRIGLEY AND HUNT **The John O' Gaunt Studio, Lancaster**
The Priory and King's Own Chapel Lancaster, Christ Church St Peter's Church St John's Church Unitarian Church Ripley Hospital Chapel Scotforth Church Skerton Wesleyan Church St Luke's, Skerton Queen Street Presbyterian Chapel St Paul's, Scotforth

Table 2: Examples of Church Stained Glass Work by Shrigley and Hunt.

Employers such as A W Hunt agreed to abide by certain rules and regulations drawn up in the indentures before taking any apprentices into his firm. The indentures dated 15 October 1879, for Alfred Parkinson Bulfield, stipulated that A W Hunt must provide lodgings, washing, medicine, medical assistance, all suitable clothes and wearing apparel fit for such as apprentice and that he should also be allowed to attend Lancaster School of Art (established 1856) for evening classes. Alfred Bulfield only served one year eight months indentureship; with Shrigley and Hunt until he became twenty-one years,[21] he had already received some other training elsewhere before joining the firm.

Apprentices continued to be trained by Shrigley and Hunt from the age of fourteen years. Many of these apprentices, once trained, remained in the firm throughout their working life. William Cragg Martin commenced a seven-year training as a glass painter in 1889. After completing his indentureship, he remained with Shrigley and Hunt until he died in 1927.[22]

'The Cohe Muffle' which Shrigley and Hunt used for firing glass until 1920 was situated in the workshops below. The workmen and craftsmen with pieces of glass worked side by side. All the glass had to be fired at once, which was rather a dangerous process and which produced an immediate and dramatic drop in temperature. It was, however, an important process and the glass emerged as a rich gold colour and was then ready to be used in stained glass work.[23]

Shrigley and Hunt's premises on Castle Hill occupied a position in the oldest part of town. Records show that the building dated as far back as 1625, when they were occupied by an East Indian merchant under the name of Rawsthorne. Forming part of these premises was 'Owen House Gate', an old property that formerly housed three of four cottages.[24]

The trade address of Shrigley and Hunt was also known as the John O' Gaunt Gate Studio, as this faced out onto the Lancaster Castle Gateway of the same name. The Studio's location linked in also with the religious history the craftsmen pieced together as they worked with stained glass and lead. The Studio was situated on the top floor of these premises, where there was plenty of light flooding into the large room that overlooked the John O' Gaunt Gateway (Figure 5). The Lancaster studio also had a London branch, which was situated at 28, John Street, Bedford Row, London. This looked after the commissions and business in the south of England.

A W Hunt died at his home - Longlands of Westbourne Road in Lancaster - in 1917, and had been associated with the firm of Shrigley and Hunt for nearly fifty years. Charles Frederick Turner, a draughtsman who had been apprenticed to the firm at the age of fourteen, assumed control for Mrs T Hunt and the family until Arthur Edward Hunt, the eldest son, returned home from the War and took control. It was after the First World War that the Shrigley and Hunt workforce was chopped down to four working artists craftsmen. When A E Hunt died in 1929, C F Turner became principal of the firm;[25] by this time, the workforce had increased to

Figure 5. Shrigley and Hunt's Office, Castle Hill, Lancaster. Their studio was at the top of the building. *Author's collection*

ten craftsmen working for the firm.

In the 1930s there was an increase in new houses constructed in Lancaster, as well as a new style of stained glass windows becoming popular in the home. This revived trade, and by 1934 there were five stained glass studios working in the town, not since the 1900s had there been such a boom in the stained glass trade in Lancaster. Even with some additional competition in nearby Morecambe, where two stained glass studios had opened[26] did not affect Shrigley and Hunt's business. They continued to make beautiful stained glass windows and also receive plenty of commissions for restoring ancient glass frescos and murals.

One important commission was for the restoration of the famous East Window in Beverley Minster, Yorkshire. C F Turner, together with a team of artists from the firm of Shrigley and Hunt, completed this in seven moths at a cost of £2,000. It was during this time also, that the firm restored the frescos in the Houses of Parliament and the twelve frescos in Manchester Town Hall by the Victorian painter Ford Maddox Brown.[27]

By 1936, the staff of Shrigley and Hunt had increased to twenty-two artists and five apprentices. Although this was an indication that trade was good, the firms export was seriously affected by high tariff charged being placed on the import of stained glass with foreign countries. A contract awarded to the firm for winning a competition in the USA worth £250 had to be cancelled on account of a sixty per cent tariff charge. The firm continued to obtain import contracts despite these setbacks.[28]

At the beginning of the Second World War, there were four stained glass studios working in Lancaster. Shrigley and Hunt moved from their old premises on Castle Hill to West Road in the late 1960s, where the name 'John O' Gaunt's Gate Studio' was still retained. But, in 1973, the premises were badly damaged by fire.[29] The firm continued for a number of years, under the directorship of Mr Joseph Fisher, until its eventual closure in the late 1970s.

Notes

1. Haward, B, *Nineteenth Century Suffolk Stained Glass.*
2. *Baines Directory,* 1825 Vol 2.
3. Edwards, M, *The Studios of Lancaster's Artists in Stained Glass Lancaster Reference Library,* PT 8726.
4. *Lancashire Evening Post,* 'Ancestral Link', Newspaper Cutting 2.7.1966 LEP Office, Preston.
5. *Universal British Directory,* 1799.

6. *Lancaster Guardian*, 'Shrigley/Williamson Partnership' 22 April 1837, Lancaster Reference Library.

7. Lancaster City Museum. James Williamson's Church Street, Lancaster.

8. Billington, R & Brownhill, J St Peter's Lancaster (Sands 1901)

9. Morecambe Town Hall. Cemetery Department. Mrs. S. Fearn.

10. Edwards, M, *The Studios of Lancaster's Artists in Stained Glass Lancaster Reference Library*, PT 8726

11. Obituary Scrapbook. 'The Late Mr A W Hunt,' *Lancaster Guardian* cutting 1917, Lancaster Reference Library.

12. Shrigley and Hunt Ledger, Lancaster Reference Library, MS 8030.

13. Correspondence dated 3 July 1991, Victoria and Albert Museum, London.

14. Woodforde, C, *English Stained Painted Glass* (Oxford University Press, 1954).

15. *Lancaster Guardian*, 'Soothing Charm of Stained Glass', 10 January 1936, Lancaster Reference Library, C3 P10.

16. Edwards, M, *The Studios of Lancaster's Artists in Stained Glass Lancaster Reference Library*, PT 8726.

17. Shrigley and Hunt Catalogue, Lancaster Reference Library, PT 8335.

18. Billington, R & Brownhill, J St Peter's Lancaster, Lancaster Reference Library.

19. Shrigley and Hunt Ledger. Indentureship A W Hunt and A Bulfield Lancaster Reference Library, MS 8030.

20. Shrigley and Hunt Ledger. Williamson Craig Martin Indentureship Lancaster Reference Library, MS 8030.

21. Edwards, M, *The Studios of Lancaster's Artists in Stained Glass Lancaster Reference Library*, PT 8726.

22. *Lancaster Guardian*, 'Soothing Charm of Stained Glass', 10 January 1936, Lancaster Reference Library, C4 P10.

23. *Lancaster Guardian*, 'Soothing Charm of Stained Glass', 10 January 1936, Lancaster Reference Library, C4 P10.

24. *Lancaster and Morecambe Suburban Directory*, 1934.

25. *Lancaster Guardian*, 'Soothing Charm of Stained Glass', 10 January 1936, Lancaster Reference Library, C4 P10.

26. *Lancaster Guardian*, 'Soothing Charm of Stained Glass', 10 January 1936, Lancaster Reference Library, C4 P10.

27. *Lancaster Guardian*, 'Cause of Blaze Probed' Front Page 23 March 1973, Lancaster Reference Library.

5. THE LANCASTER DOCTORS: THREE CASE STUDIES

by George Howson

OF THE MEDICAL PRACTITIONERS of the early and mid-eighteenth century in Lancaster, little is known. Only for Dr Henry Bracken, medical attendant to Lancaster diarist, William Stout, and sometime inmate and later governor of Lancaster Castle is some information available. It is not clear whether James Case, a surgeon executed in Lancaster for forgery in 1799, was a local man or not. Dr Barrow, a Quaker who died in 1791, clearly was until he sustained fatal injuries after falling from his bedroom window while trying to see the Town Hall clock.[1]

From the very late eighteenth century the names of the physicians and surgeons in Lancaster are available from the various trade directories published – with varying degrees of accuracy every few years. Three who appear to be among the most prominent have been chosen for this study.

Dr David Campbell, Physician, was born in Poole, Dorset, in 1749. As with many of his professional brethren he first went to the University of Leyden and subsequently to Edinburgh. He came to Lancaster in 1772 and apart from a period of three years in Kendal and Liverpool he remained in Lancaster until his death.[2] He was involved with the public life of the town from an early stage and became a member of the old unreformed Council. He held a number of offices before becoming an Alderman and finally Mayor in 1796. In medical terms his importance lies in being one of the promoters, if not the principal promoter, of the Lancaster Dispensary (Figure 1) in 1781. A report in the *Cumberland Pacquet* for 16 January, 1781,

> *We hear from Lancaster, that a meeting of the gentlemen merchants etc. in the coffee room... it was agreed upon to establish a Dispensary for furnishing the sick-poor with advice and medicines gratis... Dr Campbell, an eminent physician readily undertook the office of attending the Dispensary gratis ...*[3]

Initially, the Dispensary was in Doctor Campbell's own house in what is now Castle Park – since demolished. However, from 1785

Figure 1. The first Lancaster Dispensary, Castle Hill, Lancaster (now demolished). *Lancaster Library Collection.*

until the year after his death in 1832 the Dispensary was located in other premises still extant, on Castle Hill. Dr Campbell remained the Physician to the Dispensary until 1805 when he was replaced by Dr Whalley (who will be considered later) and Dr Binns.

Subsequent to his involvement in the Dispensary, Dr Campbell had researched and written up and published an account of a severe typhus outbreak in Lancaster in 1784 which was regarded for many years afterwards as a model of its kind.[4] Dr Campbell applied for and was appointed Visiting Physician to the new County Asylum when it opened in 1816 which involved regular attendance twice weekly. He retained this position until he retired, due to ill health, in 1831 – again he was succeeded by Dr Whalley. There was, however much more to Dr Campbell than his medical activities. The late eighteenth and early nineteenth century was the classic period of the improving agriculturalist. This was the era of the Agricultural Society, Coke of Norfolk, and, nearer to home, John Christian Curwen and Sir James Graham. Dr Campbell was part of this movement. He had a farm at Tewitfield, just north of Carnforth. He was an active and prominent member of the Lancaster Agricultural Society, formed in 1797, and was vice-chairman in 1821. He exhibited regularly at the annual show – with some success because his will mentions a 'Gold Medal from the Board of Agriculture and Six Sterling Silver Agricultural Cups'.[5] One of his colleagues in the Agricultural Society was Charles Gibson, one of the leading local gentry, Magistrate and Deputy Lieutenant of the County. He was the owner of Quernmore Park Estate and very active in local affairs. He was also the first president of the Floral and Horticultural Society.

Dr Campbell described himself as something of a Whig,[6] but this is only partially confirmed from an examination of the poll books for the period. By 1831, however, he was petitioning for the early passage of the Great Reform Bill.[7] Somewhat earlier, in 1803, Dr Campbell had been one of the principal speakers at the cross party public meeting called to set up the Lancaster Volunteers – a Home Guard precursor in face of the clear invasion threat from France. No doubt he was something of a pragmatist when it came to politics.[8]

Socially, Dr Campbell was a member of the somewhat exclusive John O'Gaunt Bowmen Club when it was founded in 1788. Perhaps this was slightly out of character, but then the eighteenth century was, in some ways, less divided by perceptions of class than the nineteenth century became. In any event, apart from the local gentry and landowners, the other members included a fellow doctor and several of the 'West Indian' Merchants. The Phillipi Club, of which Dr Campbell was also a member, was a purely social affair which was supposed to meet every evening in the *Black Horse Hotel* in Common Garden Street. The members here were leading citizens of the town, of which he was clearly one.[9] He was not, however, a member of either of the two Freemasons bodies which existed at the time.[10]

The Lancaster Medical Book Club was founded in 1823 by a number of local doctors and surgeons. Dr Campbell took the chair at the first meeting and was elected President, a position he held for the next three years. The Medical Book Club (which still exists) was partly social, but mainly for the purchase and loan of medical text books for the benefit of the member. One would imagine that by this time Dr Campbell was regarded by his professional colleagues as the 'grand old man' of Lancaster Medicine and his election to the Presidency of the Book Club little more than a formality.[11]

As one would expect from a product of the eighteenth century enlightenment, Dr Campbell was a member of the Amicable Society. This was a remarkably successful and well stocked subscription library founded in Lancaster in 1768 – again a classic development of the second half of the eighteenth century. Many other doctors, as well as clergymen, lawyers and other professional persons were also subscribers. Most of them were his friends and acquaintances.

In keeping with his Whiggish principles, which involved progress and improvement, his belief in public service and his desire to improve the lot of his fellow citizens, the passing if the *Lancaster Street Improvement Act* in 1824 gave Dr Campbell new opportunities. The unreformed Town Council (as with many other Town Councils elsewhere) had failed in its duties (probably ill-defined) to install sewers or drains to keep the streets clean and well lit. The Commissioners under the *Street Improvement Act* had all these specific duties and had the power to levy a rate to provide the necessary finance. They were active and effective. Almost inevitably the first chairman was David Campbell.[12]

When Dr Campbell died in 1832 he had been widowed for some three years. His wife was from a clergy family in Garstang. He had no children and the bulk of his quite large estate went to nephews and nieces. He had been friendly for many years with the Reverend John Manby, the Vicar of Lancaster, and was buried in St Mary's church. Two of his legacies are worthy of note. The sum of £1,000 and jewellery went to Maria Manby (the daughter of his friend) on her attainment of twenty-one years and a piece of silver plate to the Town Council. This silver had in fact been presented to Dr Campbell some six years previously by the citizens of Lancaster by way of appreciation for his services to the Town. It was a nice touch to return it.[13] It is still in safe keeping at the Town Hall.

Obituary notices in the press should always be treated with caution because they tend to emphasise the positive qualities of the deceased rather than the negative, but the comments in the *Lancaster Gazette* are worthy of reproduction.

> *In his public capacity, Dr Campbell held during a period of sixty years the most justly merited confidence of the public and in his private as well as his social life he rendered himself beloved of all who had the happiness of his acquaintance.*[14]

One can well believe it.

Christopher Johnson, Surgeon, (Figure 2) was of the generation which succeeded Dr Campbell. Born in 1782, he survived until 1866, but much of his active life covered the earlier part of the nineteenth century.

A native of Lancaster – his father also being a doctor, he was orphaned at the age of twelve years. He was apprenticed to a medical practitioner in Preston and had further education in Edinburgh.[15] He was, however, a surgeon which did not have quite the social cachet

of the physician and during our period never did. He first practised in Settle, but by 1809 he was back in Lancaster where he remained for the rest of his life. Like Dr Campbell, his interests were many and widespread. His first public appointment seems to have been in 1809 when he was appointed Surgeon to the part-time Lonsdale Local Militia – the successors to the Volunteers.[16] Probably this would not be a very onerous task, but it was a proper thing to do at the time. His fellow officers consisted almost entirely of prominent local citizens and the Surgeon's, no doubt, patriotic action would enable him to widen the circle of his friends and perhaps, without being cynical, increase his business. By 1812 he was one of the honorary surgeons at the Dispensary and this was followed in 1815 when he took a

Figure 2. Dr Christopher Johnson.
Lancaster Library Collection

leading part (with others) in setting up the House of Recovery – an early form of isolation hospital. He was appointed honorary surgeon to this institution as well.[17] He remained heavily involved until both organisations were amalgamated in 1832. He was then appointed a trustee of the combined operation and so remained until his death.

Like many of his ex-militia friends, Christopher Johnson became a member of the old unreformed Town Council. This was surely a sign of acceptance by the self-perpetuating elite who formed the Council. This culminated in his becoming Mayor in 1833. The mayor was also an *ex-officio* magistrate, but in any event he was appointed to the Borough Bench in 1835, on which he served many years.

Quite a full account of the life of Christopher Johnson appeared in the *Lancaster Guardian* in 1910. This is reproduced in full in *The Minutes of the Lancaster Medical Book Club* edited by Graham Anderson and published privately in 1997. The article demonstrates Christopher Johnson's involvement in many differing activities. Like Dr Campbell, Johnson was a Whig, or perhaps more accurately, a Liberal and was a supporter of all the controversial measures of the times, including the Repeal of the Corn Laws, Parliamentary Reform and Emancipation of the Slaves. Nevertheless he would vote for a Tory candidate if he were a local man or likely to be good for the trade of the town. Johnson was clearly a man of great energy and with a lively mind. He was interested in public health precautions against cholera and the care of lunatics. He wrote to the local paper on these topics, as well as on agricultural chemistry, under the pseudonym of 'a Fireside Farmer'. Clearly a highly approachable man, he put himself out to assist young men from the Lancaster area in pursuing a scientific career with the offer of premises for study and the supply of chemical apparatus and books – however, this phase of his life really falls outside our period.[18]

Christopher Johnson, according to the account mentioned above, must have been a largely self-taught man. He does not appear to have attended the Grammar School. He spoke or certainly read both French and Italian sufficiently well to produce printed translations of foreign works in this country. In 1813 he published a translation of a French medical work on *The Signs of Murder in New Born Children* which he dedicated to Dr Cassals, one of his colleagues at the Dispensary.[19]

Dr Johnson was very much a Lancastrian and all of his four sons attended the local Grammar School and, indeed, they in turn went on to lead useful lives.[20] In 1816 he was among those who helped to set up the Provident Savings Bank.[21] He was also involved with the foundation of the Lancaster Mechanics Institute in 1824 and became an honorary member (for past services) of the Literary Scientific and Natural History Society. Inevitably he was a subscriber to the Amicable Library, as indeed were most of his fellow doctors.[22]

In trying to assess Christopher Johnson, he does perhaps seem more of a nineteenth century creation (in every sense of the word) than Dr Campbell. It is perhaps difficult to see him hobnobbing with the gentry at a John O'Gaunt archery competition or being a regular attendee at the Phillipi Club. He would probably (and perhaps a little self-righteously) have regarded such activities as a waste of time and as an impediment to doing all sorts of more worthwhile activities. After all he was a family man with a wife and four children to support. In addition he was skilled, learned, very conscientious, well respected and well liked. Perhaps he could be regarded as one of the best examples bridging that gap between the exuberance of Georgian England and the staid sobrieties of Victorian Society. Perhaps one illustration will assist. On 28 May 1831 the usual dinner took place at the Town Hall to celebrate the King's birthday. It was clearly an uproarious affair with no less than thirty-five toasts being drunk – the nineteenth to Dr Campbell, one of the guests. The same dinner two years later with Christopher Johnson as Mayor in the chair appears to have been a much more decorous function and was reported in a much lower key.[23]

Lawson Whalley, Physician, was a member of an old established Lancaster Quaker family. He was born in 1782 and died at the early age of fifty-nine, in 1841. His mother was a member of the Lawson family, also of Lancaster, whose Quaker involvement goes back to George Fox and the seventeenth century. Lawson Whalley's father died very shortly after his son's birth in 1783.[24] He does not appear to have attended school locally and in view of his circumstances it might have been that he was sent away to the Quaker boarding school at Ackworth, near Pontefract – a not uncommon occurrence within Quaker families, including some from Lancaster. However, this was not the case.[25] In 1785 his mother re-married – to a Thomas Arthington of a banking family from Leeds. As a consequence of this union Lawson Whalley gained a half-brother, Robert Morley Arthington who subsequently became a partner in the Lancaster banking firm of Dilworth, Arthington & Birkett which collapsed with such calamitous results in 1826.[26] Notwithstanding all this, the two men remained friends, and Robert Arthington was appointed executor and trustee in his half-brother's will.

Lawson Whalley qualified as MD in Edinburgh in 1804.[27] He

returned to Lancaster and very speedily was elected as one of the honorary physicians to the Dispensary in succession to the recently resigned Dr Campbell.[28] He became a Freeman two years later – to some extent this may have been a sign of status and respectability, but more importantly it conferred a right to vote in elections. He had clearly retained good connections in Lancaster, probably through the Society of Friends, and in any case his father had been a Freeman. In 1807 he was appointed a medical officer to the Eagle Life Insurance Company[29] – an example of the early efforts of life companies to evaluate the concept of risk involving the use of mortality tables and actuarial knowledge. Dr Whalley married in 1813 – to a Quakeress, thereby avoiding the almost inevitable disownment which would have followed if he had married outside the Society of Friends.

Being a Nonconformist, Dr Whalley in general was a Whig and supported Whig candidates.[30] Indeed, from 1820 onwards, he was usually[31] the formal seconder when the Whig Parliamentary candidate was nominated. In 1831, as might be expected, he (and Dr Campbell) signed a petition seeking an early passing of the Reform Bill.[32] Prohibited by the *Test and Corporation Act* until its repeal in 1828 from seeking public elective office, he demonstrated his social responsibility and abilities in the Dispensary (as already mentioned) but also in the sounding and running of the House of Recovery in the years after 1815.[33] Such action was typical of late eighteenth and early nineteenth century Nonconformists. In Lancaster, where the Quakers were numerous and influential (out of all proportion to their actual numbers) their names appear with great regularity in connection with local charities and other bodies unaffected by the *Test and Corporation Act*. He followed Dr Campbell both as visiting physician to the County Asylum in 1831 and as second President of the Medical Book Club in 1826. By reasons of his medical qualifications and general demeanour he appears to have ranked behind Dr Campbell only, so far as his status in the town was concerned. Nevertheless, Dr Whalley could unbend. The Minutes of the Medical Book Club mention 'The party partook of an excellent supper at the expense of Dr Whalley on his being appointed Physician to the County Asylum and did not disperse till one o'clock'.[34] Dr Whalley, as one would expect, was a member of the Amicable Library and the Literary, Scientific and Natural History Society.[35] He was an active and concerned citizen and, judging by local press reports, a supporter of the disadvantaged.

Lawson Whalley was a wealthy man. At the time of his death he was the owner of a substantial landed estate of some 112 acres at Stodday, about two miles south of the town centre.[36] Some of this may well have been inherited from Mrs Arthington, his mother, who in 1807 was described as 'immensely wealthy'.[37] He also owned a house and shop property in Lancaster itself and, rather surprisingly, a pew in St Mary's church. This, however, was let. Due to his station in life, Lawson Whalley probably did not need to work. Nevertheless he continued to do so and, as we have seen, took up the appointment at the Asylum. He performed there with the greatest credit in the cholera epidemic of 1832, when he displayed both personal courage and commitment.[38]

This ownership of land and the fact that Dr Whalley was a physician rather than a surgeon (which the majority of his professional colleagues were) does seem to have put him in a rather higher social position than those colleagues. His appointment to the County Bench (when this became possible) in 1836 rather than to the Borough Bench appears to confirm this. His colleague on the former would tend to be fellow landed gentry from all over the county rather than the local worthies (like Christopher Johnson) who formed the backbone of the local Commission. This socially upward movement continued through his eldest son not only became a barrister, but also joined the Church of England. Two of his grandsons became army officers and at least one of them was active in late nineteenth century Tory politics. None of his sons were educated locally.[39] His great grandson, the last in the male line, died of wounds in a German prison hospital in 1916.

Surprisingly, no obituary of Dr Whalley can be traced in the local press. Notwithstanding that, beyond doubt he was one of Lancaster's best known and worthwhile citizens of the early nineteenth century.

Notes and References

1. Cross Fleury, *Time Honoured Lancaster*, 1891, 507.
2. *Lancaster Herald,* Obituary, 11 February 1832, Lancaster Reference Library.
3. Original in Cumbria Record Office, Carlisle. Copy Lancaster Reference Library. B886.
4. Summary B887 PT 507. Lancaster Reference Library.
5. He won prizes for winter potatoes in 1802 and 1811.
6. See obituary.
7. *Lancaster Herald*, 1 October 1831.
8. *Lancaster Gazette*, 19 July 1803.
9. Cross Fleury, *op.cit*, pp. 457, 480.
10. Lancashire County Record Office. Return of Freemasons, 1799 and 1800.
11. Anderson, G (ed), *The Minutes of the Lancaster Medical Book Club.*
12. Docton, K, *Lancaster*, Lancaster Reference Library. B91.
13. Will of David Campbell, Lancashire Record Office, W J W.

14. *Lancaster Gazette,* 4 February 1832.
15. Anderson, *op.cit.* pp.7-9.
16. *Lancaster Gazette,* 10 June 1809.
17. Minutes of House of Recovery, Lancashire Record Office, HRLI, acc.8472.
18. Anderson, pp.7-9.
19. Lancaster Reference Library.
20. Murray, A (ed), *Bibliographical Register of the Royal Grammar School, Lancaster,* Part 1.
21. *Lancaster Gazette,* 2 January 1816.
22. Records of both counties, Lancaster Reference Library.
23. *Lancaster Gazette,* June 1831 and 1833.
24. Chippendale – Genealogies of Local Families, Lancaster Reference Library.
25. Ackworth school lists. Friends House Library, London.
26. *ibid.*
27. *Lancaster Gazette,* 12 September 1804.
28. *ibid,* 4 April 1805.
29. Cross Fleury.
30. Poll Books, Lancaster Reference Library.
31. *Lancaster Gazette.*
32. *Lancaster Gazette,* 1818 onwards.
33. House of Recovery, Minutes 1815 onwards.
34. Medical Book Club, 16 January 1832, Lancashire Record Office. DDX 2192.
35. Lancaster Reference Library records.
36. Contract for sale of estate, 1841, Lancaster Reference Library.
37. Binns, Mss. Lancaster Reference Library 7055.
38. There were ninety-four deaths from cholera in the Asylum between August and October 1832. *Lancaster Gazette,* 1 December 1832. Tradition records Dr Whalley clambering over rows of coffins in the course of his duties.
39. Murray.

6. THE FOUNDING OF GREAVES METHODIST CHURCH

by Lois M R Loudin

AN APPARENT CONTRADICTION IN THE HISTORY of Methodism is that John Welsey died as he had lived, a high church Anglican. The Methodist church began as a sub-group within the Church of England and only formally separated from it after his death in 1791, though all the elements requiring that separation were in place by 1784. Wesley had set up classes of people who joined together for Bible study, prayer and worship, linked together in circuits; however, members were still expected to attend their local parish church for holy communion. There were 'itinerant' ministers and lay preachers who met together annually at 'Conference' to discuss doctrine and practices.

During the nineteenth century, there were a number of splits from what became known as the Wesleyan Methodist Connexion. These splits were caused by disagreements over church organisation rather than doctrine. Some groups came back together again in 1857 to form the United Methodist Free Churches. The other major group was the Primitive Methodist Church founded in 1811 that grew out of the 'camp meetings'. However, each of these connexions followed a similar structure of Conference, circuits and classes.[1]

Methodism in Lancaster

Before there were dedicated chapels, Methodism operated with 'preaching places'. Lancaster was originally in the Haworth circuit; in 1776 this was divided and the Colne circuit was created. Eleven years later the Blackburn circuit was formed and Lancaster formed part of this until 1794 when the Lancaster Wesleyan circuit was created. The Kendal area was taken out of this in 1805 and Morecambe and Heysham in 1894.

The first permanent preaching place in Lancaster was established in 1795 in the upper rooms of two cottages on the corner of Damside Street and Wood Street. Numbers were soon too great for this and in 1806 a larger church and minister's house was erected in Sulyard Street – then known as the Friarage. This building was enlarged in 1830 and 1836 but, again, it became too small. The Sulyard Street church was erected in 1874, providing accommodation for 1,100 worshippers, and costing £9047.

For many years, Methodist chapels had sought to reach the young through Sunday school work. The first Sunday school was established in Lancaster in 1792, and remained in the chapel buildings until 1834. It was then held in various places until in 1852 a new building was erected in Edward Street. From 1874, the Sunday school met in rooms underneath the Sulyard Street chapel until a purpose built set of rooms was erected in 1893 to form both day and Sunday school rooms and other rooms for church work at Sulyard Street. These cost £5,685.

Lancaster Methodism was affected by the splits from the original Wesleyan Connexion and eventually had three circuits based in the area: Wesleyan, Primitive and United Methodist Free Church. The Primitive Methodists had two chapels in town, Moor Lane and Skerton, while the United Methodists met in Brock Street. Mission churches were established by the Wesleyans in Bridge Lane, on the Marsh and in Westham Street.

Origins of the Greaves

According to the circular published to start the fund raising:

> It has long been recognised that some movement in the way of Methodist Extension in Lancaster is greatly needed. The population is growing and the town expanding on every side, yet Wesleyan Methodism has made no advance in Church accommodation for many years past. Whilst not unmindful of the good and faithful work of the other Churches, we feel that it is our duty to take a larger share of responsibility and of service.
>
> Last year we celebrated the Centenary of Wesley Church, and the time seems now peculiarly opportune for initiating a bold, progressive, and aggressive policy, so as to make the second Century of Lancaster Methodism even more successful than the first.
>
> Many who live in the suburbs of the town would gladly retain their connection with our Church, but find Sulyard Street is too distant to allow of regular attendance there. We are thus in danger of losing families whose sympathies are entirely with us.[2]

A site for a new church on The Greaves, on South Road, opposite Brunton House, was purchased in 1903 at a cost of £1,000 (Figure 1). The next year, a site for a new church at Skerton was bought for £700. These were paid for by subscriptions and grand bazaars held in 1905 and 1906 which raised £1,450 and £632 respectively. In

Figure 1. Map of Greaves, Lancaster.
Lancaster Library Collection

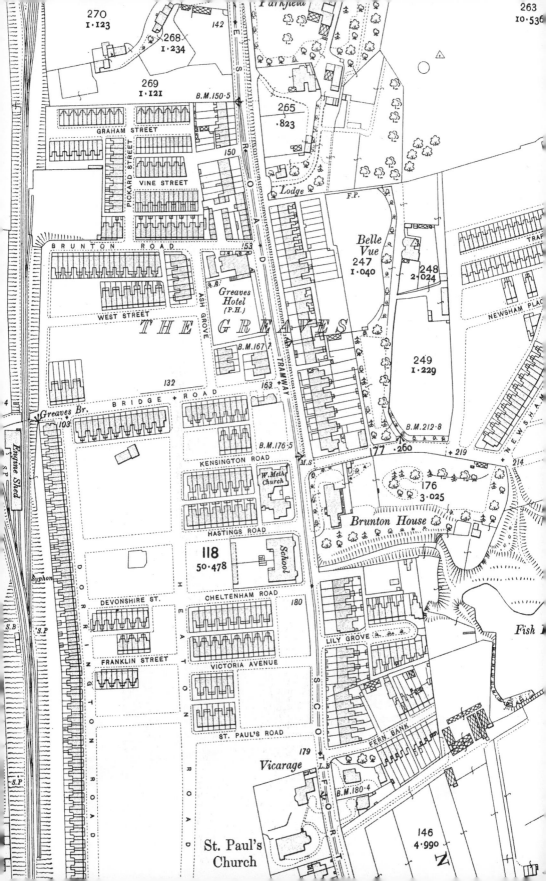

1906, the Circuit Quarterly Meeting approved a scheme to build the two churches, with their associated Sunday schools, at a total cost of £13,000. The plans for The Greaves were drawn up by Stanley Wright, then Mayor of Morecambe.

The building scheme was inaugurated by special service in Sunday 3 March 1907, at Sulyard Street, at which Reverend S T Bosward, the Superintendent Minister of the Circuit, preached. The next afternoon, a large congregation heard a sermon preached by Reverend S F Collier, Superintendent of the Manchester Mission, which was followed by tea and a short musical recital by Mr A Douthwaite, organist and choirmaster. In the evening, a public meeting was held, chaired by Alderman Norval Helme, MP. He said that,

> *While a chapel was needed at the Greaves, they did to like to leave their friends in Skerton in their old premises. Therefore, that the two projects might be proceeded with, he an his brother Robert, recognising the great interest their father took in Skerton, had decided to pay for the erection of the chapel at Skerton, estimated at £4,000.*

Also present at the meeting was Reverend John Hornabrook, Secretary of the Connexional General Chapel Committee, who commended the four thousand guineas that the Lancaster Circuit had contributed to the Twentieth Century Thanksgiving Fund, and he said that he expected the Fund might give £2,000 to the Lancaster building scheme. Other donations promised at the meeting amounted to £2,500. On this basis it was decided to implement the building programme (Figure 2).[3]

Figure 2. Proposed new church and school at Greaves. *Author's collection*

Building the Greaves

The foundation stone for the church was laid on Wednesday afternoon, 14 October 1908. The crowds stood on South Road – watching out for trams and cars – while a short service was held, led by the Reverend W J Chant, the new Superintendent Minister. The first stone was laid by the Mayor of Lancaster, Councillor Wilson. A cavity in the stone held a bottle containing a circuit plan, circuit magazine, copy of the statement of appeal, a circular announcing the ceremony, the local newspapers, a document containing the names of the trustees, etc. a photograph of the builder and his workmen and a few coins. The Mayor was presented with an engraved trowel. The other stones were laid by Mrs T D Smith (whose husband, the grocer, had been a committed Methodist), Mr John Davis (one of the oldest Methodists), and Mrs J Dugdale (wife of the junior circuit steward). The address was given by Reverend J T Wardle Stafford of Scarborough, who said,

> *There was a great need for evangelical churches in the suburbs. He heard a whisper that a church like that would take away from the old centre, but they must not take that view. It was their duty to make their own chapels more attractive. If Christian people were more enthusiastic, their town churches would be better filled... There could be no doubt that there had been a great slump in attendance at public worship. People no longer went to churches as they used to do simply because the doors were open. They were vastly more critical than they were twenty-five years ago. The motor cars which were passing along the road were an illustration of the change in the habits of the people. It would be a serious thing if the religious observances of this country were to be neglected. Gentlemen like the Mayor of Lancaster knew the value of religious efforts in the maintenance of good order, and they were erecting that church because they knew the value of the Christian life, and desired men and women to come under its religious influences and be witnesses for righteousness. It was essentially a peoples' church and they must let the people feel that it was for all of them, and they could gather there and worship unitedly. They felt increasingly that their Methodist chapels should be like homes to the people, and the more the made their church like home, the more likely would it be to succeed. He hoped that the evangelical gospel would always be proclaimed to those who gathered within the walls* (Figure 3).

Figure 3. Engraved trowel presented to the Mayor. *Author's collection*

Figure 4. A font presented by Mrs Wright, wife of the architect. *Author's collection*

Afterwards, over 500 people attended tea in the school at Sulyard Street. In the evening, there was a celebratory meeting with several speeches and choral items, and more promises of gifts, including a font from Mrs Wright, wife of the architect (Figure 4).[4]

Sunday school children in the district had been encouraged to raise money for the schoolrooms at the Greaves. Those who raised a minimum of ten shillings (50p) each laid a brick, the singing being led by the band of the Salvation Army. The Mayoress led the procession and laid the first brick in the vestibule entrance to the schools. The second was laid by Mr Chant and then the children came up in alphabetical order. The children, after laying their bricks, were presented with a white medal, which had, on one side a drawing

Figure 5a. Medal presented to the children. *Author's collection*

Figure 5b. Reverse of the Medal presented to the children. *Author's collection*

of the church and schools and on the reverse, the inscription 'The Greaves Wesleyan Methodist Church, Lancaster. Easter brick-laying ceremony, 14 April 1909'. The *Lancaster Guardian* in its account of the event listed all the children with the exact amount each had raised. Following the ceremony, everybody marched back to Sulyard Street for tea. In the evening there was a meeting at which the youngsters wore their medals and listened to speeches (Figures 5a and 5b).[5]

Opening of the Greaves

A description of the building in the *Lancaster Guardian's* account of the opening was as follows:

> *In the church itself, which occupies the northern half of the site, an adaptation of the decorated gothic style of architecture has been utilised, and at the north-east corner is a tower seventy-six feet high, with a copper turret and finial. The outer walls of the building, which has a pleasing elevation, are Lancaster stone, with dressings of Darley Dale, and the windows, which are of stone with traceried heads, are glazed with leaded lights of a very pale green shade. There are two main entrances, both from South Road, with the inscriptions cut into the stone arched over-doors. 'Enter into His gates with thanksgiving' over the south door, and over the north door the continuation of the text 'and into His courts with praise'. A commodious vestibule in the north entrance gives access to the gallery staircase which is built into the tower. The gallery extends the full length of the western end of the*

church, which altogether provides accommodation for 600 worshippers, and is seated with substantial pitchpine open benches, stained a pleasing shade of green. A feature of the interior are the massive columns and roof timbers, which with the gallery front, have been stained walnut colour and varnished. A raised platform in the chancel provides accommodation for the communion table, the oak pulpit, and the benches for the choir, whilst the organ is located in a transept on the north side.

The schools, which occupy the southern half of the site, are arranged on the modern plan of a large central hall, with class-rooms, to the lower series of which communication is afforded by folding screens, the upper range of class-rooms being approached by a gallery with seating accommodation projecting into the school room for use in the opening and closing services. The present accommodation is for 250 scholars and teachers, but the premises are so constructed as to be capable of extension at comparatively little cost should the necessity arise. The principal room is lofty and exceedingly well-lighted, and the class rooms are commodious, airy and well-ventilated. There are separate entrances to the school which is separated from the church at the front by a spacious garden court, laid out with beds of artistic design planted with shrubs – an entirely new and pleasing feature in the church architecture of the district. At the rear of the court the premises are, however, connected by a lofty well-lighted passage, which also gives access to a series of vestries and other apartments, the construction of which was made possible by the great fall in the ground. These include a commodious parlour for the ladies' societies connected with the church, separate vestries for the minister and choir; and in the basement lofty and well-ventilated apartments for use as a school for infants, as well as a commodious admirably equipped kitchen, lavatories and cloak-rooms, and heating chamber. The kitchen is connected with the ladies' room by a lift, which will also be utilised for gatherings of a social character in the school room. Wood block floors have been provided in most of the rooms, and the passage between the church and the school is laid with duralithic wood.

The premises are heated throughout on the low pressure hot water system, but gas fires are also provided in several of the smaller rooms. The lighting is by electric current. The premises ate divided from the adjoining roads by a broad asphalted walk, and the walks of the garden court are also asphalted, the whole being surrounded by a stone balustrade with unclimbable iron rail fence. The total cost of the new premises, including the site, is about £8,500, and towards this there has been subscribed or promised nearly £6,000, leaving a little over £2,500 still to be raised (Figure 6).[6]

Figure 6. Plan of seating in the church.

Author's collection

WESLEYAN METHODIST CHURCH,
THE GREAVES,
LANCASTER.

PLAN OF SEATING

SCALE OF FEET.

FEET 0   10   20 FEET

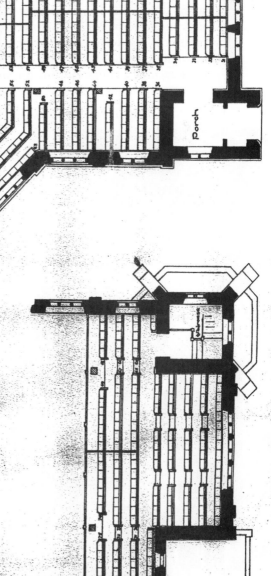

Plan of Church

Plan of Church Gallery

ORGAN

Choir

Choir

Tower Porch

Porch

The opening ceremony was held on Wednesday 13 October 1909. Just as the ceremony was due to start, there was a heavy shower, so the ceremony had to be held indoor. Mrs Pratt of the Woodlands, Silverdale, unlocked the northeast door and a big crowd followed her into the church. Mr Chant, the Superintendent Minister, announced that the church had been registered as a place of worship by the Register General. The service of dedication was led by the President of the Wesleyan Methodist Conference, Reverend W Perkins, who preached a sermon. Hymn singing was led by the Sulyard Street Choir, conducted by Mr A Douthwaite, with Miss E O Brash at the harmonium. Following the service, tea was provided in the schoolroom for about five hundred.

In the evening a public meeting was held in the church. (Figure 7). Among the speeches, information was given by Mr Chant on the

Figure 7. Greaves Church. *Author's collection*

progress of the building fund. He reported that a total of £5,830 had been raised leaving £2,600 still to be found. He also commented on the way that the free churches in town worked together and thanked the new vicar of Lancaster for his brotherly spirit. The president of Conference referred to a previous president, Reverend Hugh Price Hughes, who

> had insisted upon the importance of three great words – liberty, education, regeneration. They wanted liberty – freedom of every kind – but they wanted education that liberty might be enlightened and guided to right issues; and they wanted regeneration, the application of the gospel of Jesus Christ and the power of the Spirit of God to the hearts and lives of people. It was their duty as in days gone by to preach the necessity for a great change. The 'new birth' was not a dream; they had not outgrown sin and because of that there was still the necessity for regeneration, the salvation which was in Jesus Christ, which would change the hearts of men, reform their lives, take away their passions, give them a new disposition and enable them to break away from their old habits of sin and indulgence. He was jealous that they should have a warm welcome for the poor weary souls that wanted pointing to the way of salvation. They were looking for a great revival, but what they wanted was a deeper stronger conscientiousness, a more real sense of duty in the service of God. There was nothing God honoured so much as obedience, and when people became conscientious to the spirit of duty, God would look upon them with favour and blessing.[7]

Establishing the Greaves

Reverend Edwin Bell was appointed to the Circuit, with pastoral responsibility for The Greaves, and established in the existing manse at 3 Sea View, almost opposite the church. (A new manse was acquired in Skerton). In January 1910, membership was forty-five. (Sulyard Street having dropped from 287 to 248). Within a year of the opening there were seventy members. Thereafter the rise was slower, reaching 100 in 1919.

Services were held on Sundays at 10.30 am and 6.30 pm and on Thursday evenings there was a prayer meeting at 7.30 pm followed by a preaching service at 8.00 pm. The first two baptisms on 24 October 1909 were of Bernard James Gorst and Kathleen Amy Warwick. The Sunday school was opened on 17 October 1909 by Mrs Helme of Springfield Hall, with 157 scholars enrolled.

Society and Poor Stewards were appointed initially by Sulyard

Street Church Council. The two Society stewards were Mr George Millington and Mr John Forsyth; and the two Poor Stewards, Mr Thomas Parrington and Mr Christopher Hodgson. The Greaves minister appointed as Chapel Stewards Mr W Clough and Mr Edward Gorrill. Class Leaders were appointed: Joseph Smith Gorrill and John Lawrence. Kirton transfereed from Wesley Society and Joseph Forster Lightfoot was the new leader. At the first leaders' meeting on Thursday 28 October 1909, the times of the class meetings were decided. Junior classes were held on Thursday evenings at 6.30pm by Mr Lightfoot and Mrs Crossley. Mothers' meetings were held on Monday afternoons and a series of Saturday concerts organised. Later, there were evening literary meetings, and a Bible Class for men on Saturday afternoons.

A Coronation Bazaar was held in the Town Hall from 29 March, daily until 1 April 1911, in order to raise the funds to pay off the debt of the Church. £1,5000 was raised. After the debt was paid off, the next need was for an organ. A three-day bazaar was held in 1923 to raise the funds to replace the small manually blown harmonium. The new organ was installed in April 1923 and in the same month, the stained glass windows were added.

In this way, a new Wesleyan Methodist Church was established.

Notes and References

1. Tabraham, Barrie, *The Making of Methodism*, Epworth Press, 1995.
2. Lancaster Wesleyan Methodist Circuit, Church Building Scheme, CRO Mla 1/7/14.
3. Methodist Recorder 'Great Church Building Scheme at Lancaster', 14 March 1907.
4. *Lancaster Guardian*, 'Wesleyan Extension Scheme: New Church on Greaves: Laying the Memorial Stones', 17 October 1908.
5. *Lancaster Guardian,* 'Greaves Wesleyan Church Lancaster: Unique Ceremonial', 17 April 1909.
6. *Lancaster Guardian*, 'Greaves Wesley Church', 9 October 1909.
7. *Lancaster Guardian*, 'Wesleyan Progress: New Greaves Church opened: Visit of the President', 16 October 1909.

7. THE DUKE'S THEATRE

by Bernard Gladstone

THE DUKES THEATRE AND CINEMA situated in Moor Lane, was originally St Anne's church, built in 1795 by the Reverend Robert Housman, great-great-grandfather of the poet, A E Housman (Figure 1). Converting the church into a theatre was quite appropriate due to its history.

The Reverend Robert Housman started his career as staunchly Church of England. However, his beliefs turned more towards Methodism at a time when this was extremely unpopular. Consequently, he found it increasingly difficult to find churches where he could preach, as most Church of England parishes barred their doors to him. In 1793, the Reverend Robert Housman returned

Figure 1. Dukes Theatre, Lancaster, formerly St Anne's church. *Author's collection*

to his home town of Lancaster to build his own church where he could preach his own brand of religion.

Lancaster at that time was strictly Church of England, and although the Reverend Robert was not a true Methodist as such, his Methodist leanings made him very unpopular. The Church was known as 'The Hot Bed of Dissent', and there was much political and religious infighting in Lancaster to try to prevent the church being a success. The Reverend Robert persevered with his idea and, at the time of his death, had been vicar of St Anne's church for forty-one years. By this time, in contrast to its beginnings, St Anne's had one of the biggest and most thriving congregations in the city, and the Reverend Robert had become one of the most respected members of the local community.

Reverend Robert Housman's success in building up his congregation and changing the attitudes of the city towards him can, perhaps, be put down to his early pulpit training. He learnt his pulpit style from the great actor, David Garrick, and it was not only the content, but also the theatrical manner and fervour with which he delivered his sermons that made him such a popular preacher.

St Anne's church was thus established in Lancaster against a background of mixed feelings and some downright opposition. Over the years, partly because of his theatricality, and partly because of his approach and beliefs, the Reverend Robert overcame the initial obstacles and his 'Hot Bed of Dissent' became a most respected and important part of the community.

Around 176 years later, the Dukes opened its doors for the first time in similarly controversial style. A great deal of time, effort and money went into bringing to fruition the plans for a civic theatre for Lancaster. Those whose faith in the project had remained unshaken had to face criticism not only from the many who liked to go 'agin the government' on principle, but also from some who had genuine doubts as to the wisdom of such a venture. Pessimists pointed out that a number of attempts to introduce repertory theatre into Lancaster had failed, but the last was more than a decade previously and local conditions had changed considerably in that time. There had been a marked cultural stimulus locally due to the advent of the University and College of Education, and the potential of support for a theatre was considerable. Those in charge of the venture were fully aware of the possibilities of the watershed in a wide area to the east and north where opportunities of seeing live drama were non-existent.

Discussion for the formation of a civic theatre was initially led by the City Council during the Second World War. A municipal theatre was included in the list of buildings that they wished to acquire in their post war development plans. Unfortunately, the scheme was swamped by much more pressing needs for several years.

In 1962, a general development plan prepared by the City Architect included a civic theatre that was to be sited on the north side of Dalton Square, on the space occupied by the former County Cinema. The projected opening date was 1982. From 1963 to 1967, protracted negotiations took place between the city council, the University of Lancaster, and Lancaster Footlights Club. The plan was to convert Lancaster's Grand Theatre, owned by the Footlights and which was built in 1781, into a civic theatre. There were disadvantages to this plan, as the Grand is a traditional Proscenium Arch type theatre, which it was thought would hamper flexibility in presentation, and its seating capacity of 571 would be difficult to run economically.

In 1967, Century Theatre approached the city council with an alternative plan. Century was a touring theatre, which trundled thousands of miles around the country bringing theatre to towns that had no cultural centre. They toured their theatre trailers, each thirty-three feet long, which were lined up side by side. Hinged panels forming the sides of these trailers were folded downwards to provide the sloping floor of the auditorium. Wall panels filled the gaps in the side to complete a solid weatherproof theatre with under floor heating and 255 upholstered tip-up-seats. The stage was twenty-five feet wide and nineteen feet deep, and was fully equipped with up-to-date lighting and sound equipment. It also included a bar and foyer, workshop, dressing rooms, offices, laundry and living accommodations. It was designed to be erected by a team of eight men in a day and was moved from town to town by members of the company aided by volunteers.

Since it began its working life in 1952, Century Theatre had had a hand in the opening and development of many new theatres, gaining invaluable experience and contact with both town and county theatre-goers. They had visited Lancaster on several occasions, citing their theatre on the lorry park at the top end of Thurnham Street. They were anxious to establish a permanent base from which to tour and the plan was to convert St Anne's church to a 300-seat theatre with additional facilities added on available space on the north and east sides of the building. It was though that the proportions of St Anne's church, and its simple, sturdy stone construction, would make it ideal for conversion to a theatre of the right size.

Figure 2 and 3. Before being turned into a theatre, the building was used as a warehouse. *Lancaster Library collection*

The building had ceased to be a practising church in 1959, when it was bought by the Council. They at first used it as a warehouse, until the plans for a civic theatre came to fruition (Figures 2 and 3).

Work on the conversion commenced on 3 November 1970. Very simply, the conversion took place by taking a bulldozer from one end of St Anne's church to the other, leaving one end wall, two side walls, and the roof of the church intact. The conversion then took place inside the shell. The stage and raked seating take up roughly the area that was taken up by the altar, organ loft and pews, and the foyer takes up the space that was originally the old entrance to the church. As the seating is racked at the back of the auditorium where the seating gets up quite high, this combines with the space where the old entrance was, and forms quite a spacious foyer. The lighting equipment above the audience is suspended from the old beams of the church, and the external features of the church have been kept intact, and, indeed, the building in many ways has been renovated and cleaned as far as the exterior is concerned.

From the beginning, it was intended that the Dukes would offer more than a straight repertory programme. To that end, the plans for the conversion included provision for film projection, and, utilizing vacant land to the east end of the church, a second smaller auditorium (the studio theatre) was built to be used for experimental productions, children's theatre, and other forms of work that could not easily be accommodated within the main auditorium. Support areas around these performance areas include dressing rooms, wardrobe and laundry facilities, and a scene dock and office accommodations.

The Lancaster city architect, in consultation with Century Theatre was responsible for the design, and Thomas & Jackson of St Anne's Place, Lancaster, were the main contractors. The success of the enterprise was achieved with help of grants and aid from the City of Lancaster, the Arts Council of Great Britain, the British Film Institute, the Gulbenkian Foundation, the Pilgrim Trust, Lancaster University, and many commercial and industrial firms.

All this was achieved in exactly twelve months, and on 3 November 1971, Mr A W Jackson, Director of the form which built the Theatre, handed over the keys to the Mayor of Lancaster (Councillor Mrs Winifred Sweeney), who presented them to Alderman Doug Clift, Chairman of the Century Theatre Management Committee. Alderman Clift, in this opening speech, said that when he was told twelve months previously that the Playhouse would be opened on 3 November, he never thought that it would be ready in the exact date. He thought that it was a tribute to the men who had built the Playhouse, and what really was pleasing was that the company responsible, and most of the workers, were from Lancaster. The building was described by the Mayor as a realisation of the city council's wish to have in Lancaster a living arts centre where drama, films, music and exhibitions would all be equally at home. Following the opening ceremony, the film Private Road was shown to an invited audience.

At 8 o'clock on the evening of 29 November 1971, an actor called Russell Denton said 'Call m Ishmael', and Lancaster really believed that it had a repertory theatre. The first production was *Moby Dick*, directed by Century Theatre's Peter Oyston, based on the script for Orson Welles's film of the Melville epic. It ran for a week, and played to an audience that was just seventeen per cent of the building's capacity, but was artistically well received.

Century continued its association with the Dukes for the next six months, presenting plays and films on the main auditorium, while in the studio the Young People's Theatre Company was providing a theatre-in-education service to children from primary to sixth-form level. But in July 1972, Century Theatre ceased to run the Playhouse. The split was by mutual agreement, and came as a result of an inability to reconcile the two activities that Century was committed too. Namely, touring theatreless regions in its unique mobile theatre, and establishing a regional base in Lancaster. It was thought to be more logical and economical to have two companies, each with its own special purpose. A new company was formed to run the Playhouse independent of the city council, but consisting of a mainly Lancaster based Board of Directors. Personnel who were currently working in the Duke's Playhouse continued to do so, and the new company undertook responsibility for all contracts entered into in respect of the Duke's Playhouse by the Century Theatre. The Finance and Policy Committee of the City of Lancaster recommended that a grant be paid to Century to assist in the payment of creditors and to discharge the Duke's Playhouse from all liability to Century Theatre, and so the association came to an end.

Lancaster had not had a professional theatre for twenty years and therefore, since the opening, the Theatre had been engaged in the sloe process of building up a policy and an audience in an area with no established theatre-going habit. The process was intensely slow. The first season played to only thirty per cent capacity, but over the next two years this figure rose to eighty per cent. A firm theatre base had been established in Lancaster.

In 1976, in order to reach a wider audience, the Dukes started producing the occasional small-scale tour, visiting village halls, community centres and schools. Also in that year, the Duke's embarked on a new venture, acquiring the lease to the Theatre on the Central Pier at Morecambe, setting their sights on producing top class theatre for visitors during the summer months. In order to ensure the best, the first task was to improve conditions in the theatre for patrons. The worst seats, from which it would be difficult to see or hear, were removed. A new stage was built, the bar renewed, and the box office was improved. Finally, the theatre was painted inside and out, even the roof was painted in bright red and yellow stripes. The benefit for the Duke's was that for the first time continuous employment was possible throughout the year. Traditionally, the theatre had gone dark during the summer months. Sadly, the venture did not attract sufficient audience numbers, and after only two seasons the project came to an end.

The Young People's Theatre which was established soon after the Dukes opened, began this type of work under and agreement with the old County authority, when a grant was made available to cover part of the costs, the remainder being made by the Arts Council. The Education Committee were told that the Arts Council had since made a distinction between 'Young People's Theatre' – production intended for children – and 'Drama Education' – work done in schools by theatre companies. The Education Committee approved the appointment of four actor/teachers and technicians to enable more work to be done in schools. So, the Duke's Theatre-in-Education was born, and over the next twenty years, established a fine reputation for highly esteemed work, which meant a lot to both the pupils and teachers in primary and secondary schools in Lancaster, Morecambe and throughout the country. All their good work came to an end in 1995, when Lancashire County Council ceased all funding for theatre-in-education at the Dukes.

The Lancaster Youth Theatre commenced at the same time as theatre-in-education, and for the first couple of years met in the Dukes Studio. Then, in 1977, they moved their base to a converted brewery building at the rear of the Duke's Playhouse, known as 'the Bottleshop'. The Youth Theatre catered for a wide range of ages, and covered all aspects of art and drama, several members going on to become professional actors. In August 1994, whiles closed for the summer break, the Bottleshop was completely destroyed by a savage fire, leaving the Youth Theatre homeless. One year later, the Duke's Theatre received a Lottery Grant to convert the derelict Primitive

Methodist church in Moor Lane into a new Youth Arts Centre. Work on the conversion began in January 1996. The centre opened on 8 November of that year.

The studio space at the Duke's had been unable to be used for some considerable time. It was decided in 1980, to make this space a 'theatre-in-the-round', thus providing a second and very different auditorium. Theatre-in-the-round had its origins in medieval street theatre and strolling players. In the sophisticated form of modern theatre building technology in this country it had been recognised as an alternative form of staging only since the 1940s, with the building of places such as the Questor's Theatre, Ealing (not totally in the round), and the pioneering work of men like the last Stephen Joseph at Scarborough. The Duke's Theatre in the round was constructed from scaffolding and timber with seating in a series of three levels. By the elimination of scenery, and the fact that the actors had to play knowing that at any time some of the audience are at the back of them, and through consequent intensification of their relationship with the audience, it created a very exciting new experience for Lancaster audiences.

Although the Duke's now had two auditoria the soundproofing between the two was woefully inadequate, and meant that restrictions had to be made on the number of productions and events in each season. Any even in the studio disturbed the theatre and film audiences in the main auditorium, and vice versa. This problem was not solved until 1994, with the installation of proper soundproofing thanks to generous financial support from Lancaster City Council, and the Foundation for Sports and Arts.

In the main auditorium, all the early productions were done on the traditional style stage, but in 1986, came a dramatic change with the advent of the thrust stage. This gave a greater acting area, and more flexibility in the design of sets. Every design though, has to allow space for the cinema screen to come in for film nights.

The Duke's Cinema – or the Lancaster Film Theatre as it was originally known – has been in existence throughout the Duke's life, and has shown thousands of screenings over the years. Films are booked through various distributors, including City Screen and the British Film Institute, and shown on the biggest screen in the region. Stalwarts of the cinema will remember the period when the heating system failed and customers were provided with blankets to keep out the cold. In 2001, came the introduction of 'Big Noise Special'. This is a state-of-the-art ex-Digital sound system comprising of four 100 watt speakers on each side of the auditorium, four along the back

Figure 4. Ashton Memorial in Williamson Park, Lancaster. *Author's collection*

wall, and three 1200 watt speakers behind the screen, and a 1600 watt bass bin under the stage. This far exceeds what most other venues have, and gives a much clearer and more subtle sound, being able to cope with extremes of loudness and quietness, whiles still maintaining clarity of sound.

Going back to the theatre side of the Duke's, plays in the first fifteen years had consisted on in-house productions, small-scale tours, and joint ventures with other theatres. In 1985, however, came a new venture – the Promenades. These started with a production of *The Winters Tale*, in the Nuffield Theatre at Lancaster University. The success of this prompted various lighthearted discussions as to where a promenade could be mounted outdoors, but the idea was not taken seriously until it was realised that the Ashton Memorial in Williamson Park was being renovated, and would be opened in the summer of 1987. The Dukes approaches the City Council, and discussed the feasibility of putting on a play in the park. It was decided to do a promenade version of *A Midsummer Nights Dream*. Then came a six-month production headache mobilising a massive team of people to prepare the park for the event. Power, water, drainage, and telephones were non-existent in the park, and these problems had to be overcome, in addition to providing the normal facilities like seating, food, drink, and toilets which audiences expect. There were huge obstacles to be overcome, but the work of the staff, the support of the Council, and the amazing spirit of the actors, technicians, and volunteers turned what could have been a disaster into a huge success.

Over the years, the Duke's Promenade Season has established itself as one of the highlights of summer in the north west. Each year more people come to watch the magic performances as they unfold in the beauty of Williamson Park (Figure 4). Each year new locations are sought, and new ways to use old locations are found. Thousands of people have been introduced to this unique (copied, but never beaten!) theatrical environment, and have gone away marvelling at the excellence of the spectacle.

It is now thirty years since the Dukes opened, and in that time they have produced over 260 plays, in addition to playing host to numerous tours by other theatre companies, the Litfest, the Maritime Festival, the Folklore Fiesta, cabarets, Startrek evenings, senior citizen talent contests, quiz nights, and the Storytelling Circle.

8. A Spirited Leap into the Unknown

by Graham K Dugdale

EVERYBODY LOVES A GHOST STORY. To experience that chilled ripple of fear racing down the spine both excites and terrifies simultaneously. Yet only a tiny minority are prepared to admit that they believe in things that go bump in the night, unless of course, it's next door's gate banging again. We all scoff at such notions, passing them off as the product of an over-active imagination, a result of one too many at the local pub, or the darkness playing tricks on the mind.

During the hours of daylight, such tales pale into insignificance being merely an adjunct to wile away a sunny afternoon on the golf course. But how many of us could claim a similar nonchalant attitude when hurrying home alone through a gloomy wood as nightfall rapidly enfolds the landscape in its sinister embrace. Wind moaning through swaying branches suddenly assumes the cry of some tormented soul; trees take on sub-human form as their twisted shadows attack the imagination conjuring up all manner of bizarre connotations. Sweaty palms, and a quickening heartbeat are only calmed when the reality of a familiar world stifles these eerie sensations.

This deep-rooted nervous reaction to the unknown was brought home to me as a child when visiting Madam Tussaud's Waxwork Museum in London. In those days, brave and hardy adventurers were challenged to spend a night alone locked in the infamous Chamber of Horrors. Successful accomplishment was rewarded with the princely sum of £50. Few if any appear to have succeeded in completing the task; such is the power of the subconscious manipulations of the concrete world.

Even as we enter the new millennium, the potent force of imagination is never far from the surface where strange and enigmatic happenings are concerned. Paranormal investigators frequently assert that they have been able to scientifically prove the existence of previously illusive phenomena. And still we remain sceptical assuring ourselves that it was all some trick of the light, to climatic vagaries causing the sudden drop in temperature. Until some bizarre ghoul leaps out of a cupboard to literally grab our attention, so it is likely to remain.

With a historical tradition stretching back into the depths of a hazy past, it may come as no surprise that all manner is legends have grown up to enhance the hypnotic attraction of Lancaster and its surrounding area. The element of the town's past is now working to its distinct disadvantage in the form of enhanced tourist facilities.

In the not too distant past, an image of 'dark satanic mills' combined with the grim picture of terraced streets depicted by the paintbrush of L S Lowry was dominant. Today, ghost walks conducted around the city centre are a popular feature that add a certain piquancy to Lancaster's fascinating heritage.

Intrigue and mystery will always stimulate heated debate, none more so than when fact and fantasy merge together. Many of the colourful villages around Lancaster conceal a myriad of secrets that have evolved over time. Passed down through generation by word of mouth, such fables are often difficult to repudiate.

Mystical tales held a mesmeric fascination for Lancastrians. And doubtless the arrival of the mail coach from distant parts back in the late eighteenth century encouraged locals to exaggerate the otherwise mundane into grandiose exploits. Held spellbound beneath flickering candlelight by the eloquent rendition of strange happenings, travellers were more than willing to slake the storyteller's thirst at the local hostelry in exchange for a magnetic evening of ghostly entertainment. Scribbled down at some point by an astute correspondent, they have been handed down for posterity to judge the truth of their content.

Lancaster and its environs have played host to a wide range of strange and unusual events involving ghosts that drift effortlessly along gloom corridors, apparitions that appear as if from nowhere then vanish just as quickly, together with a complete array of weird and wonderful spooks that all too frequently have their origins at the bottom of an empty tankard.

There is no doubt that all the best stories concerning a ghostly presence have at least part of their origins based on historical fact. When people who are known to have existed come back from beyond the grave, their haunting presence is all the more poignant and believable. There are numerous stately homes in the locality where these apparitions have been experiences.

One of these is Borwick Hall (Figure 1), to the north of Lancaster. Once a noble country seat, it now acts as a residential outdoor pursuits centre under the control of Lancashire County Council. Although the central pele tower dates from the fourteenth century when such dour blockhouses were necessary for protection against

Figure 1. Borwick Hall. *Author's collection*

marauding bands of insurgents, the main period of Borwick Hall's glory began in the 1590s.

It was Richard Bindloss who expanded the gracious residence accrued from profits in the trading of Kendal cloth. As a royalist sympathiser, the third Sir Robert provided a haven for the future King Charles II after the crown fell to Cromwell's parliamentary army. Here it was that in 1651, the young prince dreamed of winning back his father's crown prior to fleeing into exile on the continent.

During his brief sojourn at Borwick, Charles tarried awhile with a local girl which led to its inevitable conclusion. He left soon after. But following his restoration to the throne, Charles remembered the product of his dalliance and made full provision for the child's future.

Most sinister of the Bindloss retainers was the family chaplain who refused to cut his beard after Charles I was executed in 1649. Richard Sherlock exercised an unhealthy influence over Sir Robert who was induced to overtly persecute the 'New Puritanism' by breaking up meetings and abusing the participants. Although the

Lord of the Manor was said to be 'rich as any man in the north', he fell in with malign company which proved his undoing. No doubt his continued support of the Royalist cause did nothing to improve his fortunes and thereafter, Borwick Hall fell on hard times.

With regard to the mysterious element that has long emanated from the grey walls, we must return to its inception and the rascally Thomas Whittington. This callous rogue attempted to force his daughter into marrying a 'suitable husband' of his choosing. Her persistent refusal incensed Whittington who imprisoned his wayward daughter in the high tower. And here it was that she remained, opting for a slow death from starvation rather than succumbing to her father heinous demands.

Known as 'The White Lady', the poor girl's ghost is said to wander the corridors of the pele tower searching for a means to escape from her incarceration. Even though most visitors have no knowledge of the legend, frequent sightings of the mystical figure clothed in white and sporting a wistful expression have been reported.

To the south of Lancaster lies Thurnham Hall (Figure 2), which

Figure 2. The old chapel attached to Thurnham Hall, south of Lancaster. *Author's collection*

dates from the thirteenth century. Occupied by the local Dalton family for 450 years, it fell into disrepair when they stumbled upon hard times. In 1973, it was acquired by Stanley Crabtree of Rochdale who restored the property to its former glory through an extensive programme of refurbishment. A task accompanied with panache, the owner had managed to retain the authentic flavour of the original house now transformed into a thriving time-share complex.

Oldest of the ghosts believed to haunt the corridors of Thurnham Hall is a Cavalier from the period of the Civil War. Thought to be a certain Colonel Thomas Dalton, he has been observed dashing along the upper landing of the house. For what reason and whether he was astride a snorting charge at the time has never been revealed.

Elizabeth Dalton was the lady of the house during the middle years of the nineteenth century, and it was she who added to the distinctive chapel extension in 1845. Her ghost has been sighted on numerous occasions, walking through her old bedroom clad in a green dress. It seem fairly certain that this the enigmatic young woman who was witnessed in recent years 'floating' across the lawn in front of the chapel. Said to be wearing garments like those of a nun, she simply vanished into the trees.

Last of the trio, a somewhat impish boggart is said to have scattered the sticks laid in the fireplace. Snatching bedclothes of slumbering guests is also thought to have been one of his tricks. Jessica Lofthouse, the eminent Lancashire folklore expert, said that a boggart

Could be sly, full of mischievous pranks, his nuisance value high. But he rarely did serious harm and was often helpful in the 'good brownie' family tradition in that he was usually tolerated.

As 'made' fires and bedding have largely given way to central heating and duvets, it would appear that this particular boggart has been inactive for some considerable time. Maybe the intense human activity surrounding the Hall might today encourage the spirited little rascal to resume his antics.

At the entrance to Thurnham Hall stands the cottage where the last of the Dalton, Miss Alzira Eloise lived until her death in 1983. Staunchly Catholic in their religious leanings, the Dalton family chapel was replaced in 1848 by the 'inspired' church that now beckons the faithful to the parish. Isolated amidst the sprawling trees of Thurnham estate, one can only speculate as to why such a grandiose structure was created in this outlandish position.

One of the numerous villages lining the broad sweep of the Lune

Figure 3. A trio of ghosts reside at Melling Hall in the Lune Valley. *Author's collection*

Valley, Melling (Figure 3) straddles the main road evoking a poignant nostalgia for a more gentrified age. Such was a time when the horse-drawn mail coach announced its arrival with a fanfare on the posthorn, and cattle were driven to market along the main thoroughfare. Today, cottages of dressed sandstone weathered to a rustic hue would most certainly assure Melling a place in the elite ranking of villages were it not for the busy main road.

Melling Hall is located at the eastern end of the village where the road constricts appreciably, forcing the traffic to slow at the bend. It is indeed a miracle that more accident have not occurred with card ending up in the lounge bar. Not the most auspicious method of reserving a table for dinner.

Nearby, the solid resolute church of St Wilfrid has enjoyed a chequered history stretching back to the fourteenth century. One of its most significant features is the underground passage that connects with Melling Hall. Now blocked off for safety reasons, its original purpose remains a secret, although an escape route for defiant Catholic priests and their followers during the Reformation of the sixteenth century seems most likely. The Hall itself was originally owned by the Darlington family, its Georgian façade having been extended at various intervals.

During the First World War, Lady Darlington did much to alleviate the suffering of troops wounded on the western front. The Hall was transformed into a convalescent home and was in such great demand that another was opened further along the main street. It was not until some years later that the first intimation of a ghostly presence was reported in one of the guest rooms after the building had become a hotel. A lady dressed in purple was seen combing her hair in front of the dressing table mirror.

When the landlady narrated this bizarre happening to an old villager, she was informed that Lady Darlington frequently wore a gown of just such a colour. Nobody who spends a night in the Hall should walk in fear of such a spectre which had clearly undertaken such munificent works for the benefit of the wider community.

Another curiously quaint appearance concerns a little man who is said to jump about on the beds in a state of fervid excitement. Only three feet tall with a triangular face and pointed nose, his legs have been reversed with knees at the rear. Whosoever admitted to having been heckled by this breezy leprechaun had doubtless been exercising his arm in the bar downstairs. Either that or my leg is being pulled.

Last of the trio on offer at Melling Hall relates to a dog often heard padding softly in the upper rooms. Investigation has predictably revealed nothing, not even the proverbial church mouse. Perhaps both of these rascally phantoms had made use of the secret passage endeavouring to fool us all.

Two miles to the west lies the village of Hornby. One correspondent made the witty observation that the designer of Hornby Castle might well had possessed a touch of Disney magic in his blood. And driving along the Lune Valley from Lancaster, one can certainly accede to such an opinion.

But a fairytale castle beloved of Disney, it is not. Defensively situated within a band of the River Wenning and protected by steep cliffs, it has been utilised by generations of settlers in search for a safe base from which to operate. The Viking warrior Horni, who gave his name to the village, was one of the numerous warlords to appreciate the protective nature of the site.

After repulsing the incursions of various invaders, the castle earned a well-deserved reputation as an impregnable stronghold. Ensconced within a ring of trees, the best views is from Hornby Bridge where it spans the River Wenning. During the Civil War in the seventeenth century, the castle was heavily fortified by Royalist troops and all assaults by the Parliamentary forces were repulsed with vigour. According to reports of the day, 'unscalable precipices' defended the eastern approaches of the steadfast redoubt. In consequence, this flank was left unmanned, all available soldiers being concentrated at the vulnerable side.

Colonel Assheton was in command of the Roundhead besiegers. At a loss as to how the castle could be taken, he was approached by a local sympathiser who knew of a secret way up to the steep buttress. A cunning plan was duly hatched and put into operation.

Whilst Assheton led a distracting frontal assault, the main force accompanied their guide up the cliff route. Too late, the Royalist garrison realised their predicament. Quickly overrun by the attacking forces, the castle was given no option but to surrender.

So relieved was Oliver Cromwell when he heard the news that such a crusty carbuncle had been lanced, he gave orders that 'the Castle of Hornby be forthwith so defaced, or demolished, that the enemy may be prevented from making any further use thereof ...' Its days of resistance to the new government were well and truly numbered.

Along the main street of Hornby lies St Margaret's Church (Figure 4).

Figure 4. St Margaret's Church, Hornby. An unusual tower with eight sides. *Author's collection*

Unusual in design, the octagonal tower clearly has a much more ancient pedigree than the rest of the building. There was even a church on the site in Saxon times. The tower was built by Edward Stanley after he had been accorded the eminent title of Lord Monteagle, Knight of the Garter. This was a reward from Henry VIII following a Scottish rout at the Battle of Flodden Field in 1513.

Stanley's intention to complete the church was unfortunately interrupted by his untimely demise in 1824. As a contemporary rhyme elicits

> *The beauteous tower and alter then appear'd*
> *But Stanley died before the Church was rear'd*

His remains were interred within the ground of Hornby Priory that stood on an elevated dias on the River Lune to the West of the village. A temporary measure only until such time as the noble lord could be laid to rest in the church. But a royal decree thwarted this last wish.

Henry ordered the Dissolution of the Monasteries when they refused to condone his right to a divorce. Hornby Priory was amongst those religious houses that were desecrated and destroyed. Today it has been replaced by a somewhat innocuous farm with no indication that a priory ever stood there.

Nor is there any evidence that Monteagle was ever re-interred within the new church according to the stipulations in his will or that a monument to his memory was erected. Indeed, it is thought that the ageing bones of the great man lie somewhere beneath the hallowed ground near Priory Farm. Is it any wonder that strange sightings have been reported over the years?

Mystery and paranormal activity have long been a feature of Lancaster itself. Within the portals of its historic past, numerous aspects of a splendid heritage remain unexplained and open to debate even in today's hi-tech age. This facet is vigorously encouraged by the continued popularity of the regular ghost trail organised by 'Cat Walks' around the City Centre.

It should come as no surprise that the nucleus of psychic experience hovers around the ancient site of Castle Hill. Gruesome tales of murder and dark intrigue have long permeated the walls of the grim castle, which was the principal law courts for the whole of Lancashire until recent times. Many are the trips that have set out from John O'Gaunt's Gateway passing down Church Street and up Moor Lane to the site of execution atop the Moor itself at Golgotha.

Figure 5. *The Golden Lion*, Moor Lane, Lancaster. *Author's collection*

The tradition was to pause at the *Golden Lion Inn* (Figure 5) where the condemned were offered a final tankard of ale.

One of these unfortunates still haunts the cellar of the pub and is thought to have been a teetotal saddler who refused his last drink. Too late, the man learned that he had been reprieved. By the time the messenger arrived, the poor chap was swinging on the gallows. Another ghost seen at the *Gold Lion* is said to be one of the Pendle Witches. She was observed climbing slowly up the cellar steps and has been blamed for beer barrels emptying themselves, leaking pipes and self-pulling pumps.

Perhaps the most renowned element of cabalistic endeavour surrounds the trial and execution of the Lancashire Witches that took place in 1612. Certainly no figment of licentious imagination, the so-called witches struck fearful awe into the minds of an ignorant populace.

All manner of strange denouncements flitted back and forth between the accused. And even after their final journey to the place of execution, stories regarding their mystical powers have drifted down through the centuries to strike terror into the hearts and minds of young and old alike.

It is not the place of this article to enquire into the already well documented sequence of events that led to this most captivating slant on Lancaster's history, merely to point out that in these murky times it was rather too easy for such speculative phenomena to be accepted at face value.

News travelled slowly and was often distorted with the telling. Folk medicine was dispensed by quack doctors who claimed a host of mystifying remedies accepted gratefully by a simple populace that rarely travelled far. Fear of God and the church ensured that many 'satanic intrigue' was bound to be exaggerated out of all proportion.

The arcane is ever more alarming than anything tangible and will in consequence engender a fear that spreads like cancer choking off any attempted explanation. Through the ages, witchcraft has always incensed people making them less tolerant of stereotypes, usually old women living alone who were perceived to be infected with the 'devil's mark.' Nobody wanted the finger of denunciation pointing at them and so were more than ready to accuse others.

Yet spectral happenings are not automatically the preserve of a less enlightened period. In November, 1983,[1] a prison warder at the castle almost bumped into what he thought was a ghost on the tower steps. It was dressed in a white shirt and brown trousers and sported a ginger beard. The duo stared at each other for a full minute before the apparition finally vanished. Other employees a the prison later confirmed that they had likewise experienced similar visitations but of differing appearances. A dancing girl, judge, serving wench, pirate and small girl have all been reported at the same spot.

Adjacent to the castle stand the ancient priory, which has itself been the subject of spooky machinations. Two tramps once arrived in Lancaster and decided to spend the night there in preference to the strict control exerted at the causal ward of the workhouse. Settling down for the night, one of them thought of the rich pickings to be lifted. He could be off early the next morning and sell the loot in exchange in a life of ease.

Waking up in the middle of the night, the thief crept up to the altar where gold plate and candlesticks were in abundance. Soon after, a terrifying scream woke his partner. Seeing his colleague was missing, the tramp went to investigate only to find him dead on the alter steps clutching a candlestick, his face contorted into an agonised grimace.

One ghost that has continually reappeared over the ages is supposedly a 'friendly' spectre who has haunted, if that is the right word, the art gallery on Cheapside since 1720.[2] He is reported to smell of lavender and tobacco smoke, ruffling hair and breathing heavily. Nobody was frightened of this particular apparition until some years ago a second 'visitor' arrived which proceeded to move pictures, shut doors causing an eerie sensation that was reckoned to be a threat to the friendly ghost. Further investigation revealed that a man had once murdered his wife in the building. On being apprehended and found guilty, he was hanged within the castle walls.

One of the finest buildings in the city and still in regular use is the Grand Theatre on St Leonardgate (Figure 6). Now owned and run by the Footlights drama group, it was first inaugurated by Austin and Whitlock who operated a number of northern theatres back in 1782. Charles Dickens and Paganini are known to have trod the famous boards at one time. One particular actress who has been resurrected at frequent intervals is Sarah Siddons whose brother-in-law managed the theatre for some years. Sarah was even seen by the late Pat

Figure 6. The Grand Theatre, Lancaster. The ghost of Sarah Siddons haunts the theatre. *Author's collection*

Phoenix who performed here with a repertory company in the 1950s.

One particular night a watchman employed at the Grand shrugged off these stories of ghostly visitations as being of little consequence. And for two years nothing happened to change his view that such things were all in the mind. Then one night whilst an electrician was working on the stage lighting, the watchman decided to eat his supper in the auditorium for a change.

He sensed a presence floating down the aisle towards the stage. It was a woman with a smile on her pale face. She appeared through a door beside the stage. From that day on, the man never scoffed at anything paranormal again. He claimed to have seen the floating lady once more in the theatre before he retired. Other people have had things thrown at them and one person who described the phantom later found that it bore a striking similarity to the picture of Sarah Siddons, which hangs in the theatre.[3]

The most recent paranormal experience that I have come across relates to the old Conservative Club (Figure 7) in Church Street. Here it was, in a back room, that Bonnie Prince Charlie dined on 25 November 1745, whilst on his way south during the Jacobean uprising. The food would have been prepared in the kitchens below

Figure 7. The Old Conservative Club in Church Street, Lancaster. *Author's collection*

adjacent to the beer cellar. And it is here that a steward hurrying to change a barrel perceived a nebulous figure at the far end. The secretary of the Conservative Club recalled that 'People have heard singing behind this door when no-one was there.'[4]

Leading investigators into psychic phenomena, Melanie Warren and Tony Wall assure us that 'ghosts are alive and well and living in northern England!' Sceptics, however, are more than likely to question any existence of ghostly activity, claiming that it is rarely if ever repeated. The aim of the paranormal investigator must be to determine the elements that lead to sightings and occurrences that are often referred to as 'hauntings.'

Only then can we begin to unravel the unexplained mysteries that have baffled successive generations through the ages. Paranormal research has attempted with some degree of success to solve these nebulous conundrums by embracing scientific methodology.

It has been suggested that the increased level of public interest shown in astrology and the paranormal is a backlash against a push-button society that has resulted from today's hi-tech revolution. But whatever your own personal views on the subject, there can be no denying the charismatic appeal that stories connected with mysterious happenings engender. Thomas Hood made the point with poetic eloquence in this brief yet poignant excerpt from *The Haunted House:*

> *O'er all there hung a shadow and a fear;*
> *A sense of mystery the spirit daunted,*
> *And said plain as whisper in the ear,*
> *The place is haunted.*

Notes and References

1. *Prison Service News*, February 1991.
2. *The Visitor*, 18 October 1978, article by Harry Kite.
3. *Dominion*, First newsletter of the Arcane Gothic Society, 2000.
4. *Lancaster Guardian*, 10 March 2000, article by Judith Dornan.

9. Some Water-Power Sites in the Lancaster Area

by P J Hudson

QUITE WHEN WATER-POWER from the streams and rivers adjoining Lancaster in the Quernmore Forest and Township commons areas was brought into use is not known for certain. There are no pre-eleventh century references to any mills in the area, but the immediate post-Conquest period seems a likely time for the foundation of permanent water-powered corn and fulling mills. Recent field surveys and other research by the writer has located several sites where there is evidence of water power being harnessed to run corn grinding and fulling mills.[1]

For the early mills the documentary evidence is very sparse. Very little can be found about the history of these mill sites, who established, built and ran them, where they got their supplies and materials from and who their customers were. Even when looking at the later eighteenth and nineteenth century sites there are few surviving account books, or any other documents connected with these types of mills. It has also been difficult to find reliable primary written evidence for any of the ancillary activities which could be tied in with particular sites, eg. millstone making,[2] smithying, wrighting or building and maintenance work (Figure 1).

Figure 1. Some water-powered sites in the Lancaster area. *Author's collection*

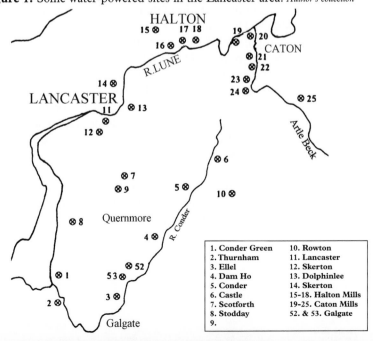

1. Conder Green	10. Rowton
2. Thurnham	11. Lancaster
3. Ellel	12. Skerton
4. Dam Ho	13. Dolphinlee
5. Conder	14. Skerton
6. Castle	15-18. Halton Mills
7. Scotforth	19-25. Caton Mills
8. Stodday	52. & 53. Galgate
9.	

No mills are recorded in the Lancaster area in the *Domesday Book* – the earliest dates for mills working in the town and villages are Lancaster Mills 1149,[3] Aldcliffe Mill 1150,[4] Stodday,[5] Ellel 1240,[6] Caton 1251,[7] Dolphinlee 1290,[8] Conder Mill 1475,[9] and Scotforth Mill is not mentioned until the late seventeenth century, in 1681.[10] In the medieval period all adjoining vills and manors had established their own corn mills, most of which were subject to the mulcture, with the exception of Lancaster, where in 1193 the township had bought its release from Count John's suit of his mills.[11]

The Norse, or Greek, is the earliest known type of watermill. The type has a long history and was recorded in use in the hill regions of the eastern Mediterranean for some 3000 years.[12] Norse-type mills have horizontal wheels and fixed vertical drive shafts so differing from the modern types, the Vitruvian. The latter have vertical wheels and horizontal drives through cog-wheels and gearings.[13] The Norse types were small, easy to erect near any source of quick flowing water, gill becks or hill streams being more use than a sluggish lowland river. Not much power was produced so the grinding stone was small and slow, but quite adequate for local farm use and for grinding small quantities of grain on demand. Norse mills had a wide range in medieval Europe and were used in the Lake District.[14] There is one watermill mentioned at Buttermere dating before 1215,[15] and is considered by Marshall and Davis-Shiel (1966) to be of the Norse type.[16]

Horizontal water wheels were still in use in the nineteenth century in the Shetlands, the Faroe Islands, and Iceland, with some 500 being recorded. One was recorded still in use at Sandness, Shetland in 1933 by Derry & Williams (1960). Tucker (1972) located some information on these mills but found there was no corpus of research material available.[17] The subject of horizontal mills in Britain is discussed in a pamphlet by Wilson (1960).[18]

Lythe Brow 'Norse' mill at SD 521 619 in north-east Quernmore, is marked on the six-inch Ordnance Survey map as 'Roman Kiln'. This structure was investigated by G M Leather and others,[19] in the 1960s and 1970s, without drawing any conclusions or finding any reliable dating material. A recent brief field inspection and some recording has come to the following tentative interpretation of this site. It is, possibly, a 'Norse-Type' water powered site[20] or a later medieval water mill of similar design.

The site is right down in the valley bottom alongside the main drainage stream and is subject to flooding in normal rainfall conditions: not a situation that would be chosen by anyone needing

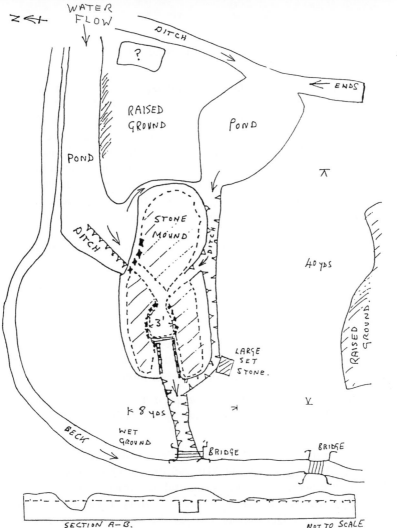

Figure 2. The 'Norse' Mill site at Lythe, Quernmore. *Author's collection*

to occupy the site for other than making use of the readily available water supply. The design and construction of the site, seen in the present remains, exhibit all the characteristics associated with waterpower use.[21] Site characteristics are very similar, in some respects, to the Davies Farm site discussed below. The main remains consist of a long mound with some surviving coursed and loose stonework. At the west end there is an opening with coursed stones and a channel with a small 3ft (0.9m) square water-filled chamber set back into the mound. This small chamber is very like the chambers constructed to take the small horizontal paddle wheel in Norse-type water mills. Other pertinent features are marked on the site in plan (Figure 2).[22]

The earliest documentation of water-powered sites in the area outside Lancaster Town refers to sites on the Royal Forest area and commons in present-day Caton-Quernmore and can be found in the land grants of Cockersands Abbey, in Caton and the Forest Attachment Rolls of the Verderers Court for 1290-92, and other contemporary legal documents. As the mills were an important source of income these records usually reference 'mills', 'millers', and 'fullers' working in the manors or, as is the case in the Lancaster district, in the Royal Forest lands adjoining villages where they held granted land.

There was a grant to the monks of Cockersands Abbey by Herbert de Ellal of

> ...*a fulling mill on the Conder between Linholme and fishery, for fulling their cloths... and no others to full cloths there, and they cannot erect any other kind of mill there.*[23]

There are one or two items on the Forest Eyre Attachment Rolls and the Master Forester's Accounts referring to corn grinding 'mills', for example Fines at Swanimote of 1478-80, show that

> *Christopher Petchet holds of the miller of Conder one pyche in the water there and it obstructs the water course and disturbs the fishing, ordered to remove it 2d. fine.*[24]

The 'miller of Conder', must refer to Petchet or others operating the Conder Mill situated at SD 510 595 on the Quernmore township border with Scotforth.[25] This was a mill presumed to have been used by both townships. In the seventeenth century it was the main corn grinding mill for Quernmore, outside the vaccary farms, for by this time Scotforth Township had its own corn mill and windmill sited in Scotforth village at SD 486 599.

Conder Mill has a long history, probably subject to several phases of rebuilding, and more recently, in the mid-nineteenth century, it was here that J Bibby and Sons of Liverpool had their origins, through Edward Bibby, the firm's founder. He was the son of a miller in Wyresdale[26] and served his milling apprenticeship there. He later worked at Milnthorpe Mill, before taking the tenancy of Conder Mill at the age of forty-one, in 1820.[27] The mill was purchased by him in 1830 for £1,450, with a £1,000 mortgage (Figure 3). At this time it was a three-storey mill of stone and slate with adjacent mill house and thirty-acre farm. The family/owners of the site changed their trading name to J Bibby & Son in 1878 with premises in Lancaster in Fleet Street (the Steam Mills).[28] The Conder Mill building was

Figure 3. Reconstruction sketch of Bibby's Conder Mill. *Author's collection*

destroyed by fire on 1 July 1885,[29] and not rebuilt, but the adjoining houses still survive, as does the farm. Edward's son, James Bibby, lived on the site until his death on 2 July 1897, aged eighty-five. No mill building or machinery survives, but the millpond fed by a headrace from the Conder remains and there is a culverted leet under the road and several millstones preserved in the front yard.

A plan by Peter Jackson dated 1815,[30] drawn when the new pond was added to the water works, names the owner as William B Bradshaw, Lord of Halton Manor, who must have died in this year as the second set of drawings which include the changes, state it is

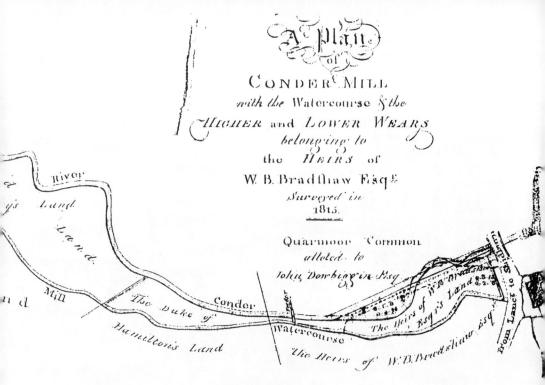

Figure 4. A plan of Conder Mill by Peter Jackson. *Author's collection*

for the heirs of William B Bradshaw of Halton (Figure 4). The site is marked on the 1845 edition six-inch Ordnance Survey Map as Conder Flour Mill (disused). This is not correct as the site was in use as a corn and provender mill at this date by James Bibby.[31]

First reliable mention of any water-powered corn mill site so named in 'Quernmore Township' is in the early seventeenth century at Rooten or Rowton. There is also a reference to an old mill being pulled down in 1726, this event being recorded in *Lancaster Corporation Minute Book D:*

> *Thomas Hewetson is given five pounds by Lancaster Corporation for the mill pulled down in Quernmore if he delivered up the lease from the town, dated thirteenth Oct 1726'.*[32] *The site if this mill is lost, but it could have been either one of the surviving 'illegal' mills for which there are no extant records, or it could be a mill given as a gift to a monastic house in the medieval period.*

On the Ellel-Quernmore boundary there are the remains of a water mill layout just below Dam House Bridge at SD 4985 5770.[33] Here there is a well-preserved water race on the west bank of the Conder which starts downstream of the bridge and runs for some 200 metres to a place where there are some stone remains, mainly cobbled ramp like features, but no trace of building foundations. Dam Head, the name of a property upstream from the bridge, suggests some sort of link with a water mill site. Investigation of the upstream area has found nothing surviving that could be interpreted as a dam or ponded area connected to the remains of a water race that starts just downstream of Dam House Bridge at SD 500 576. This was probably the site of the thirteenth century fulling mill mentioned above.

A mill in Quernmore was advertised for sale in the early nineteenth century as '...a water corn mill of the bankrupts Robert Allinson and John Whitaker...[34]',[35] this might have been the Conder Mill, technically in Scotforth. The sale could refer to the water mill at Rowten (SD 525 594), which is situated on part of the old 'vaccary' lands occupied as cow farms from the late twelfth century, so it was on a well-established settlement site which would possibly have needed a corn mill from the late medieval period in order to function as a viable unit. The evidence from the last building on the site indicated that it was of seventeenth century date: a bank mill of two storeys with a projecting porch and a flagged roof, now converted to a dwelling house. No machinery remains on the site, only a millstone, and a race culverted under the building and a stone-lined tailrace running parallel to the Rowton Beck down to the main road. There is a drained pond some 500 metres to the north east at SD 528 597 connected by a headrace, with traces of a further headrace up past Fell End to take water from Trough Brook at SD 534 604 about one kilometre away. This old headrace, which had a double channelled ponding area at SD 531 602, is now dissected by the old road up to Fell End farm, one of the vaccary land extensions, which is presumed to date from the thirteenth century.[36] This road is well worn down into the land, evidence that the building of this headrace must either pre-date the road, or has crossed it via a launder when a water flow was needed at the mill. The mill wheel was probably overshot and small, not producing more than 10hp. This would appear to be an anomaly; why did such a seemingly unimportant mill have such a large, extensive water collection and distribution system, most of which was situated on common land? The building was not in use as a mill when the Morris family held part of the land in the late nineteenth century, but they kept up the pool to the north and built a small island in it for ducks, and it is still used today.

Old photographs of this mill in the Robert Moss collection[37] show no datestone,[38] only an old millstone in front of the dilapidated building. Further surveys of the site found two small ponds in woods upstream and connected works to take water off Rowton Beck via a weir and sluice at SD 5281 5918. This race then ran down the north side of Rowton Brook Gill via a stone flag lined race. All other connecting water works near to the mill building and its pond have been destroyed by Thirlmere Aqueduct works in the 1890s. A Map dated 1806, of William Jepson's lands, by W Hall, shows the mill as Rootenbrock Mill, with all water works intact.[39]

There is a mystery about this site as there are no records of the Rowton Mill ever being worked, before or after this date, nor are there any records of a miller to be found in the township/parish records, Wills or any other primary source documents that the author has seen. It is known that the Jepson family owned the site and Rootenbrook Farm[40] from the early seventeenth century,[41] until 1822, but there is no record of them operating as corn millers on the site either.[42] There is only some brief information on the occupants in the Census returns.[43]

There was another mill site further south at Booth Hall Farm, variously called 'Theybothe Fall'[44] and 'Rothfall' in some documents. A survey of the site found only the drained depression of the pond, which was fed by a series of springs, which a culverted water channel, in the field to the rear of the present farm building range. The dates for this mill are rather vague, but it was on a site which has an ancient farmstead dating from before 1541.[45] However, the mill is not named in any documents found before a lease of 1825,[46] when the farm was let to John Dickinson. The old farmstead site and the mill was demolished when the farm was remodelled; the new farmhouse and buildings being erected in the late nineteenth century, when the name changed again to Booth Fall.[47] The name was changed again to Booth Hall in this century, c1930.[48]

Another site where there is fragmentary field evidence for water-power use is at present-day Days Farm in north Quernmore. Like Booth Fall, this is now a farm site, and has been renamed several times in its long history. On one map dated 1760 the site is called 'Websters',[49] and it also had some field place names connected with textiles, eg. 'tenters'. This site presents something of a problem. Named 'Colliers Gate' in the late eighteenth century, in connection with the coal mining activities to the east, and the site is connected by a metalled road (which was the Caton-Quernmore boundary bank) to known coal pits.[50] However, the site appears to have incurred a name change several times depending on the type of economic activity that was being carried on in the buildings or nearby.

In the Park Hall survey of 1669 this site is referred to as Drayes

Barn. But on the earliest known map of the area, dated c1760, the site name is different. This map shows three buildings and is called 'Webster's Farm'. It is, at this time, part of the Quernmore Park Estate of the Hon Lord Hugh Clifford. The site at this time was probably used for hand-loom weaving and as a small farm; a dual-occupation site commonly found in this period of pre-industrial development. In the early thirteenth century this is possibly the site of the Caton fulling mill as it is on Eskewbeck and adjoins the 'Stocksbrigge' (ie. fulling stocks) mentioned in the 1225-28 bounds. The field name evidence on this map backs up this premise, as there is a 'Tenter Close' and a 'Yarn Croft' attached to the farm's land and a relict tenter bank on the north side of the beck. Field inspection shows some evidence of another tenter to the south of the beck, and use of water power from Deys Beck, which appears to have been used as a ponded headrace upstream from the road bridge. There is some possible ground disturbance and traces of building foundations in Tenters Field and in the field to one side.[51]

A later map c1800, names the site as 'Days Barn', but on the First Edition six-inch Ordnance Survey map of 1842 it is called 'Collier Gate', and also on the estate map of 1842, evidence, perhaps of the later coal mining phase. On a later Quernmore Park map the site reverts back to 'Days Barn' and then 'Deys Farm', the name it has today. There are now only two sets of buildings on the site, one either side of the main Quernmore-Caton road. The present farmhouse on the west side appears to be converted from four separate back-to-back cottages, now much altered. The southern end is possibly the remains of the original fulling site and the late seventeenth century mull and farmhouse/cottage, or a hand-loom weaving site.

As to the water-power works, the bridge, roadway and adjoining field corners were altered by the County Council in the late 1960s as part of a road improvement scheme,[52] so the ponding evidence has gone along with at least one old building that was recorded on the c1760 estate map, and with it any traces of the 'coal connection' or the presumed water power works.[53]

The south gable end of the much altered house still abuts the beck which is shown on the c1760 Quernmore Park map with another small building marked upstream just across the Quernmore-Caton road.[54] There is one further problem with this site; if the new interpretation of the 1225-28 perambulations of the Quernmore-Caton bounds postulated above are correct, then this site is on Escow Beck, so named in the perambulations. This would make this site a possible fulling mill mentioned in several of the Cockersands

Figure 5. Castle Mill, Quernmore. *Author's collection*

lands grants.[55] There is also a weak outline of some type of building across the road to the south.

There is good documentary evidence for the last water-powered corn mill site to be built in Quernmore, one that was built in the steam era; this is the Cast Mill or Castle Mill at SD 520 609, which was erected in part of the common land allocated by the enclosure act of 1811 (Figure 5).

Castle Mill is a purpose built water-powered corn mill built in c1817, by one Richard Whittingham, a corn dealer, of Lancaster and the Isle of Man.[56] (This site has been surveyed and researched and is not discussed in detail here as it has been recently published, including the scale drawings updated by the writer and photographs by James Price).

It is assumed that there was at this time an increase in the growing of cereals in the Lancaster/Quernmore area after the last of the common land was enclosed and improved. So perhaps there was increased demand for corn-milling facilities, for it is known that there were two other mills in the township, plus Conder Mill and some estate-operated mills, eg. at Quernmore Park Hall Farm.[57] There were other corn mills, some of which at this time were idle or converted to other uses, at Caton, Gresgarth, Dolphinlee, Scotforth, Ellel, Bulk, Lancaster, Skerton and Halton, all within some four miles radius of Lancaster Town. In the eighteenth-nineteenth centuries there were at least three horse mills also recorded in the Quernmore valley, at Aksews, Gresgarth Home Farm and Narr Lodge (Figure 6), and another in the town of Lancaster. During the same period there were also several windmills nearby.[58]

What then assisted the final demise of these water-powered enterprises, particularly as some of the well-established local mills were refitting to use steam power to remain economic, was probably the import of cheaper cereals and the changing farming practices of the area which move over to a livestock-grassland system. Other sites changed their use – the following corn mills had either closed or had been converted to other uses by this time, eg. textiles and bobbin making at Caton, while Gresgarth, Ellel, Lancaster, Bulk and Dolphinlee, were all thought to have been closed down as corn mills by 1817.

There appears to have been some local friction and dispute about the building of this new Castle Mill. Initially, there were water supply problems at Castle Mill; and a law suit with Bradshaw of Halton, who was also owner of Conder Mill, on right to extract water from

Figure 6. Remains of horse gin at Narr Lodge *Author's collection*

the River Conder and its feeder streams. The Conder Mill took water from the River Conder further downstream. This dispute was not settled for seven years.[59]

There is still the puzzle of the lost site of the mill destroyed in 1726 as mentioned previously, and another, as yet unsolved problem, for in this area was the Monks of St Leonard's Hospital mill. The monks are reputed to have had a water mill in Quernmore Forest and this site upstream of Castle Mill, is close enough to Lancaster to be a possible location for this early grant by Count John, in 1200.[60] There is some evidence of old enclosed land which pre-dates the 1817 award adjoining the nineteenth century Castle Mill site. However, there are water works upstream from the present Castle Mill building which are not necessarily connected with the coal mining activity, and these could be connected with the layout of the new mill site which may have altered after the water rights dispute was settled.

Within the bounds of the Lancaster Forest, commons and present-day Quernmore township there are at least another four ancient watermill sites to the east, the Gresgarth mill at SD 532 632; the Caton Willow Mill[61] at SD 530 664 and possibly one other in Caton Vill; also one mill of unknown date at Littledale Hall at SD 569 621. Two further mills are recorded on the west side of Davies Farm at SD 503 632 and at Dolphinlee, but not yet located (plus the Deys Farm/Websters site already discussed above).

The Davies Farm site, on the west bank of Denny Beck, at SD 503 632, has features which indicate a water mill site used for either corn grinding or fulling, and could well be one of the Frith Brook Mills mentioned in the medieval forest records.[62] The farm site, which stands on the flat, very low lying land by the beck, has been altered in recent years with the surviving barns being converted to a modern loose housing system. The old farmhouse and other building have gone and can only be seen as stone foundations on the north, downstream of the present buildings. The mill building was situated on a mound on the north end, downstream of the site, where there is a well-preserved stone culvert, once part of the tailrace. South of this feature is a mound, with some stone fragments on it, but it has been extensively robbed of its stone. Between the mound and the old building range is what appears to be a partly-filled pond which must have been fed from the springs running from the higher land to the west and possibly via a sluice taking water from the Denny Beck upstream of the farm buildings, where there is a hint of an old walled shallow pond. The headrace is culverted under the farmstead. On the west of the lower pond there is a deep-cut channel which must have been used to run surplus water round the filed-in pond area. An estate map of the Dalton's land in Bulk dated c1800[63] shows the ponded area and the small building that once stood on the mound. This site could also be a 'Norse' horizontal type of design.

Charles Gibson, who improved the Park Estate from c1794, installed a water-power set of farm machinery in the new range of farm buildings, and details of these are recorded in the Estate Auction Sale documents in 1842. This could be similar to the system of the same period at Cragg Hall Farm, Ellel.[64] Gibson created a large lake, on the higher ground to the south west below The Knotts (to supply water). The lake supplied a smaller feeder pond behind the mill building via a stone-lined culvert. A field survey confirmed this arrangement, though the works have gone and the site is now derelict. There is further evidence to suggest that the present relict features associated with this farm water power could have been pre-dated by earlier works on a smaller scale, or even be unconnected as part of another water site. These earlier works have been located in the area of Well Wood and High Style, near SD 512 628. To the south of High Style building is the old park wall, much of which is possibly new build of sixteenth or seventeenth century date. It has been replaced in part with some new walling which appears to enclosed a wet hollow area which has a culverted drain running out on its eastern side, which is connected to a ditch running by Well Wood; this feature is then lost. Further to the south of Well Wood, on the hillside, is a large pond which appears to be connected via a sunken stone drain to the walled feature by High Style.

The old mill recorded at Dolphinlee also has very little surviving documentary evidence. The miller, Richard, is recorded for an offence in the Forest Eyre of 1290.[65] Several references to Dolphinlee occur in the Duchy of Lancaster records and in the Parish Registers but neither record a corn mill or miller. However, a map of Robert Dalton's land in the area c1816, shows field names of Mill Dam Meadow and Mill Parrock to the south of the hamlet and north of Ridge Farm, with a stream or 'race' line on an east-west axis. Inspection of the site proved to be disappointing as the hamlet with its farms, Dolphinlee house,[66] buildings and old pond, and the mill, have been destroyed by the building of the M6, the prison farms and the later farm improvements.

The same applies to the site of any water mill in Bulk vill as this area has been devastated by the building of the M6 motorway works; the turnpike road and recent road widening; the building of the *Post House Hotel;* and the farmstead of Hudson's Farm. Most of the other buildings have either been pulled down or recently renovated into modern houses. What remains untouched of this historic site is to the west, which shows evidence of the old roadway, possibly Roman, the pinfold, some old building foundations and the small crofts and tofts, which are now all under threat from development into an industrial estate.

To conclude, it is possible to deduce from the above evidence that the hinterland to the east of Lancaster mainly in what was the Quernmore Forest area adjoining Lancaster was of importance as the place where suitable water-powered sites could be installed on demand as the technology evolved to utilise this primary renewable resource evolved. However, mills are resource site specific, and one which perhaps only the forest area could provide, and when exploited this could have been for the benefit of Lancaster township, most of the inhabitants of the farms and the surrounding vills, thus, making the leap forward from muscle or horse power.

Notes and References

1. Hudson, P J, *Landscape and Economic Development of Quernmore Forest, Lancaster: An Upland Marginal Area in North West Lancashire to c1850.* Unpublished M.Phil. thesis, University of Lancaster, 1994.

2. Hudson, P J, 'Old Mills, Gritstone Quarries and Millstone Making in the Forest of Lancaster', in *Contrebis* Vol. XV, 1989, pp.35-64.

3. Farrer, W, 'Lancashire Pipe Rolls'. *Chetham Society* 1902, 298; Charter of Ranulf Earl of Chester to the priory confirming their liberties, dated 27 July, 1149, gives them a right of some emoluments of the mill at Lancaster.

4. Lancaster Charters, 37. The Abbot and convent of Sees made a grant to Gilbert to be able to raise the causeway of his pond on their land at Aldcliffe, fee of ONE POUND OF PEPPER annually, he granted them the tithes of his mills upon the pond and the tithe of fishes upon the pond.

5. Simpson, Rev R, *The History and Antiquities of Lancaster* (Edmondson Lancaster, 1852). p.228; reference in list of lands etc. of priory c1201. William de Lancaster gave the priory a rent of twelve pence, payable out of his mill at Stodale (Stodday) for permission to have a chapel on his manor of Esseton (Ashton).

6. Farrer, W, *The Chartulary of Cockersands Abbey*, Chetham Society, p.768, records gifts of the mulcture of the mill at Ellel of corn growing on his land from Walter de Ellel c1240 but there is a grant of c1200 for a fulling mill, see CC.V3.1.NS. vol. 56. (1905), 799.

7. Lancaster Inquests and Extents. i,184/5; Writ of 1251 has Roger de Heysham holding a third part of the fulling mill at Katon (Caton) and a third part of the water corn mill worth forty shillings yearly: (p.224 same entry for 1259), and Roger Gernet, master forester holds a third, and same forty shillings.

8. Eyre of 1290: Richard of Dolfineleye the miller cut down alders in a sparrow hawk eyry and destroyed the eyre in the forest of Quernmore, presented taken to the castle by G of Clifton the sheriff and delivered to prison, and mainperned by his brother Alan and John of Parles.

9. Shaw, R Cunliffe, *Royal Forest of Lancaster*, (Preston, 1956), p 192. In 1475 a miller is recorded at the mill of Condor. An ancient Corn mill now a farm, once held by the Duchy of Lancaster but owned by Bradshaw of Halton in c1815 and Bibby from 1830.

10. Lancashire Record Office (L.R.O.) RCHy: Lease 15.6.1681 Thomas Reader & Thomas Curwen mentions 'barn & kiln' and 'windmillne field' in Scotforth.

11. Farrer, W., 'Lancashire Pipe Rolls', 416: Grant of Liberties by Count John to Burgesses of Lancaster twelfth June 1193 includes freedom from the suit of the mill.

12. Derry, T K. & Williams, T I, *A Short History of Technology from Earliest Times to AD 1900* (Oxford, 1960), p.250.

13. Bennett, R & Elton, J, *A History of Cornmilling.* Vols. I IV, 1898-99, and Wailes, R, *The English Windmill* (Routledge, 1954)

14. Davies-Shiel, M, *Watermills of Cumbria,* (Dalesman, 1978).

15. Cumbria Record Office. D/Lec/299a, Lucy Chartulary, No.91.

16. Marshall, J D, & Davies-Shiel, M, *Industrial Archaeology of the Lake Counties.* (David and Charles, 1969), p.52.

17. Tucker, D G, 'Windmills and Watermills in Iceland', in *Industrial Archaeology,* Vol. 9 No. 3, 1972, p.52.

18. Wilson, P N, *Watermills with Horizontal Wheels.* Society for Protection of Ancient Buildings, Booklet No. 7, 1960.

19. Leather, G M, and Webster, P V, (1988), 'The Quernmore Kilns' in Jones, G D B, and Shotter, D C, *A Roman Lancaster, Rescue Archaeology in an Historic City,* 1970-75. Brigantia Monograph.

20. Hudson, P J, 'Notes on Roman Kiln Sites in Quernmore', *Contrebis* Vol. XVIII (1993), pp.23-38.

21. Tucker, D G, (1972) *op.cit.*, 328, shows an illustration of a horizontal water mill in Iceland, which appears to be set on a mound in a crude structure and is of similar proportions to the remains surveyed at both Davies farm and Lythe Brow.

22. Hudson, P J, (1993), *op. cit.*, pp.23-38.

23. Farrer, W, (ed) *The Chartulary of Cockersands Abbey,* (Chetham Society N.S. Vol. 40, Vol. III Part 1, 1900)., 779. 1190/1220).

24. Shaw (1956) op. cit. p 191.

25. Though it must be remembered that there is another mill possibly run of the river Conder which was demolished in 1726, and the mill on Rowton Beck to the east.

26. Faithwaite's Notebook dated thirteenth August 1835, from William Bibby 5 pounds cash, rent of mill in Wyresdale. William is thought to be Edward's father.

27. Richmondshire Wills, Edward Bibby, Conder Mill, Lancaster, yeo, A, 1854.

28. Bibby, J B and C L, *A Miller's Tale, A History of J. Bibby and Sons Ltd,* Liverpool, 1978.

29. *Lancaster Gazette,* 2.7.1885, report states loss was estimated at some £2000.

30. Lancaster Reference Library. Pl 34/7 and 8.

31. L.R.O. DDHH B39 Map J Binns 1834 of Duke of Hamiltons lands, shown Conder mill and water dam, land adjoining up to Little Fell is named Bibby, to be sold as Lot 4.

32. Lancaster Parish Register: Quernmore. 1767. Baptism Ann dau. Christopher Heuston, Quernmore. 4.10.1767. The only other Hewitson named in the register who could be anywhere near Quernmore Forest is: Alice Hewitson of Scotforth died 1662, and a will dated 1662. TRS v10 will, Alice Hewetson, Scotforth, A, adm. 1662.

33. L.R.O. Map Scotforth enclosure c1816, shows a 'Waller Dam' on high ground NE of Halla Carr Road, a possible feeder to lands by Dam House and Bridge.

34. The only reference to these surnames to be found lists them as tanners and owners of property in St Leonardsgate in Lancaster. References occur to the monks of St Leonard's Leper Hospital of right to a mill, in 1324 the abbot of Sees quit-claimed the tithes on 5 acres, gardens and tithes of their mill etc (See: Reg St Mariae, MS. Fol. 45). It is interesting to note that in 1808 when the lease or ownership of Rowton Mill is for sale that there are houses situated in Leonards Gate in Lancaster included in the list of property etc., in the Allinson Whittaker bankruptcy. This begs the question is the Rowton Mill the site of the fourteenth century monks' mill which still has links with the site in the town in the nineteenth century? Some sources state that the grant of the monks mill was originally that of John c1200. 1851 Census LRO HO107/2273: There is more information which is just as confusing, but might be used to support the above monastic connection. The Census returns for 1851 list Benjamin Birkett aged 52 and one Townson aged 31 and 1 labourer, at Old Mill, with 4 acres, but in all these cases no one is listed as connected with milling. Can this mill site and its few acres of land be a relict of the old twelfth century grant of John?

35. *Lancaster Gazette,* 22.10.1808

36. Hudson, P J, 'Two Vaccaries in Quernmore' in *Lancashire History Quarterly* Vol. 3, No. 1, March 1999, pp.10-13.

37. Moss, R, *Archives.* Centre for North-West Regional Studies, Lancaster University, Bailrigg.

38. Garnett, E M, *The Dated Buildings of South Lonsdale.* Centre for North-West Regional Studies, Lancaster University, Bailrigg, 1994. Records a datestone in a doorjamb marked with T D J, 1700, for Thomas Jepson and Dorothy Cragg, married at St Michael's on Wyre 17.10.1691. Thomas dies in 1728, but he is always recorded as a yeoman, not a miller.

39. L.R.O. DDHH B28.

40. Site is not to be confused with Rowton Brook, Rooten or Rowtenbrook, which adjoin the holding as part of the vaccary farm sites.

41. A Thomas Jepson of Quernmore was assessor for the 1607 Lay Subsidy.

42. L.R.O. DDHH Box 13, map 1814, shows the mill and water race to N, but NAME is spelled 'Rawston Brook Mill' and two buildings on site.

43. 1851 Census L.R.O. HO107/2273; *op. cit*, see footnote above.

44. Richmondshire Wills, *The Record Society*, Vol. 10, 82; 'Robert Croskell of Theybothe Fall in Quernmore, A, 1564'.

45. Quernmore common dispute of 1541 names Robert Croskill of Bothefalle, and that he had built a house there (Boothfall) within last fifty years.

46. Lancaster Reference Library, MS 3297. Lease dated 14.2.1825 between Thomas Jepson Starkie of Clitheroe and John Dickinson of Quernmore of the tenement of Rothfall, a mill, kiln and barn, and the farm of Longmoor. '...messuage and tenement called Rothfall with the mill, kiln and barns and other buildings, land closes, hereditaments and premises... in Quernmore... and all that messuage and tenement called Longmoor with other buildings lands and closes there to belonging situate in Quernmoor... to 115 acres of seven yds the rood or perch, plus two allotments of twenty-five acres ... The term is for nine years from thirteenth May next at a rent of eighty-eight pounds plus fee farm and quit rents etc...'

47. There is here some further interesting information which seem to embrace mill sites, this property was once owned by the Jepsons of Rowtenbrook, and the family name element appears to survive in the owners name written in the 1825 lease, one Thomas Jepson Starkie.

48. The present owners, Kidd's, state that the deeds do not pre-date the late nineteenth century re-building. The 1844 edition of the six inch OS map shows the outline of the ponded area, as does the 1845 Tithe Award map.

49. Richmondshire Wills, *The Record Society*, Vol. 13, 274; 'Edward Webster of Quernmore, A, 1711'.

50. Hudson, P J, *Coal Mining in Lunesdale*. An introductory study of coal mining in the valley of the river Lune and its tributaries in North West England. Hudson History of Settle, 1998.

51. If the bounds of Quernmore-Caton are as suggested elsewhere in this paper, this beck, which adjoins the site is the Escow beck of the early thirteenth century, this site is a possible for a fulling mill mentioned in several of the Cockersands land grants.

52. This site has been complicated as the fieldwork located a good spread of Roman period kiln debris upstream of the road bridge.

53. A map of c1820, only shows Colliers Gate on the east side of the road, no building on the west side.

54. Hudson, P J, (1988) *op. cit.*, pp.16-17.

55. Farrer, W, *The Chartulary of Cockersands Abbey*, Chetham Society, Vol. III Part I, pp.826-883.

56. Price, J W A, 'The Castle Mill at Quernmore: a water powered mill in a rural landscape'. *Industrial Heritage*, Vol. 26, No. 4, Hudson History of Settle, Dec. 2000, pp 6-15

57. Hudson, P J, 'Some Unrecorded Water Powered Sites in Quernmore Forest, *Contrebis*, Vol. XIV, 1988, pp.13-23.

58. Hudson, P J, (1989) *op.cit.*, pp.60-64.

59. Mr Bradshaw, a London upholsterer bought Halton Mill in 1743. He then buys an interest in several other mills as he, or his heirs, are recorded as owner or part owner of mills in Ellel, Lee in Wyresdale and the Conder Mill. (e.g. A Court case in respect of Lee Mill in 1824 at Lancaster, Bibby v. Parkinson and for landlord Bardshaw. Another the same year, Richard Whittingham v. Bradshaw. Bradshaw complained Whittingham had diverted a watercourse – the river Conder above Castle Mill – causing his mill to have a water shortage at times, judgement by Bailey and Holroyyd was given in favour of Bradshaw).

60. Registers St Mariae, MS. Fol. 45, dated 1324. Has reference to the monks right to a mill, in 1324 the abbot of Sees quit-claimed the tithes on five acres, houses, gardens and tithes of their mill etc.

61. Hudson, P J and Price, J W A, *The Mills on Artle Beck*, Caton. Archive Vol. 7, Sept 1995, Lightmoor Press, Whitney, Oxon., pp.48-57.

62. Shaw (1956) *op. cit.*, 139. Attachment Rolls Forest Eyre of 1290: Richard of Dolfineleye the miller cut down alders in a sparrow hawks eyry and destroyed the eyry in the forest of Quernmore, presented to the castle by Gilbert of Clifton, the sheriff, and delivered to the prison, mainperned by his brother Alan and John of Parles.

63. Hudson, P J, 'The Lost Treasure of Dolphinlee' in *Lancashire History Quarterly*, Vol. 4, No. 1, pp.12-18.

10. THE GRANDEST MONUMENT IN ENGLAND

by Mike Whalley

THOUSAND OF MOTORISTS driving along the M6 past
Lancaster are intrigued to see a huge domed building rising
imperiously above the treetops. Certainly there is no other piece of
architecture quite as compelling as this to be found along the entire
length of the motorway. Those travellers who do decide to investigate
further are amazed when confronted by what has been described as
'the folly to end all follies... the grandest monument in England'
(Figures 1 and 2). An instant comparison with the Taj Mahal is

Figure 1. Ashton Memorial, Lancaster. *Lancaster Library Collection.*

Figure 2. Lake and fountain in Willaimson Park, Lancaster. *Lancaster Library Collection.*

Figure 3. Williamson Park's magnificent flower beds. *Lancaster Library Collection.*

irresistible, as the Ashton Memorial soars 45.7metres (150 feet) into the sky above the city. In the same way that Lancaster's magnificent ancient castle dominates the skyline to the west, the memorial commands the heights to the east, a lasting and spectacular tribute from one lonely benefactor to his family. The Ashton Memorial is set in Williamson Park, which was once acclaimed by broadcaster Richard Dimbleby, during a visit with his *Down Your Way* wireless programme, as the most beautiful in Britain.

Linoleum magnate James Williamson little realised, when he commissioned the memorial almost one hundred years ago, that as we enter the new millennium it stands today, not simply as a unique testimony to the controversial life and times of a powerful family dynasty, but as a major tourist attraction on its own right. Williamson Park (Figures 3-6) itself was created, several years before the

Figure 4. One of the ornate sets of gates, and lodges at Williamson Park. *Lancaster Library Collection.*

Figure 5. The Butterfly House at Williamson Park. *Lancaster Library Collection.*

Figure 6. The popularity of Williamson Park remains undiminished with time. *Lancaster Library Collection.*

building of the memorial, from land strewn with rock and boulders deposited during the Ice Age. Strong evidence of the glacial age, which remains to this day, generated considerable interest among observers during the dying embers of the nineteenth century.

Records show that the Lancaster Philosophical Society considered a special paper on the subject at its meeting on 25 February, 1886. It was prepared by J Stuart Sandys, and entitled *On the traces of glacial action in Willliamson Park, Lancaster.* Mr Sandys explained that the stones to be found in the park must have been brought by ice for some distance. In the light of today's intensifying deliberations about global warming, Mr Sandys proved rather prophetic in one passage, which reads

How are we to account for the strange changes in climate? Looking

back on the past winter, we may be tempted to ask: 'will the glacial period come upon us again?' I grieve to say, 'most probably, yes.' If it be not prevented by that other event when the elements shall melt with a fervent heat, this country of ours will be once more covered with ice a thousand feet thick, and Lancaster, with its cloud-topped chimney and gorgeous asylums, and solemn temples, the great gaol itself, will be pushed over, broken, ground down into impalpable powder, and distributed as boulder clay to the Cheshire plain. Dreadful fate!

It would be interesting to hear Mr Sandys's comments today.

As for James Williamson, he was born on 31 December, 1842, the fourth child of James Williamson, master painter and gilder, and his wife, Eleanor, daughter of a local innkeeper. He was educated at Lancaster Royal Grammar School and at a private school in Cheshire. With his elder brother, Thomas, he joined his father's rapidly expanding decorating business. By 1851, the operations included the manufacture of oilcloth, a development that was to earn young James a fortune (on his death he left estate valued at more than £10 million), which enabled him to make several generous gifts to his native town. By 1873 decorating has been abandoned, as the family concentrated on the manufacture of varnish and oilcloth for both tables and floors, with more than 800 men and women being employed by the firm. James Williamson senior died in 1879 after a long illness, during which time his younger son, James, emerged as the driving force. Within four years James had bought out his brother and changed the name of the company to James Williamson and Son.

Floorcloth soon became the firm's biggest success story – hessian was brought from Dundee and coated with oil at the Lune Mills factory, standing on the banks of the River Lune. From floorcloth, Williamson's progressed into linoleum, a crucial move in its continuing success story. A potent combination of aggressive marketing and intense price competition saw Williamson's overtake Lancaster's other oilcloth firms, James's business acumen ensuring it developed into the largest producer of its kind, with buoyant overseas and home sales. Williamson's was to remain the largest oilcloth factory in the world with, at its peak, a 4,000 strong workforce.

James, who remained at the helm until a week before his death in 1930, was a Lancaster town councillor, High Sheriff of Lancashire in 1885, and then MP for Lancaster from 1886 to 1895. He was created Baron Ashton for his donations to the Liberal Party, although some years later he was to transfer his allegiance to the Conservatives. James, or 'Li'le Jimmy' as he was nicknames by friend and foe alike, was married three times – to Margaret Gatey in 1869, Jessy Hulme (née Stewart) in 1880 and Mrs Florence Whalley (née Daniel) in 1909. He had two daughters by his first wife. His elder daughter, Ella, married the Hon William Peel, later Viscount and subsequently Earl Peel, who became chairman of James Williamson and Son Ltd.

Williamson Park was developed on the sites of former quarries on Lancaster Moor, the stone from which was used to build a great part of old Lancaster. Some thirty-eight acres of rough moorland were transformed into 'one of the finest natural parks in the country' by young James's father, Alderman James Williamson, and presented to the town in 1878. James senior had conceived the idea in part as a means of providing work for the men of Lancaster as a time, during the cotton famine, when unemployment was a serious problem. It was significant, perhaps, that in the park, at its highest point, was a plateau known as 'Top of Hard Times'. It was on this very spot, early in the following century that the Ashton Memorial was to be built. Eventually, Alderman Williamson paid out of his own pocket for the whole of that area to be converted into a large park, which was formally opened on 24 March, 1896, when the Duke and Duchess of York drove through it, no doubt admiring the fine ornamental lake, floral displays, shrubs and trees and intersecting winding paths leading to various beauty spots. Pretty well as it still looks today, in fact.

Young James Williamson commissioned the memorial in 1904. That was the year in which his second wife, Jessy, died. And while, officially at least, it is said the structure was a memorial to the family, sentimentalists suggest it was a wealthy and distraught husband's way of immortalising the memory of his favourite wife – Jessy. Leasing London architect of the day, Sir John Belcher, designed the structure and in 1906 a model, on show at the memorial today, was exhibited at the Royal Academy in London. The memorial was originally planned in solid stone but rising costs led to the experimental use of load bearing brick, steel joists and concrete infill behind stone cladding. However, despite the impressive appearance of the monument, this pioneering method of construction was to generate huge problems as the years rolled by, eventually posing a threat to the structure's very existence. The memorial's face is of Portland Stone with the staircases and balustrades of Cornish granite. The main steps are of Hopton Wood limestone from Derbyshire. During construction, some 300 tons of worked stone were supplied each week by the Ashton Road stoneyard in Lancaster.

The building contract was awarded to that other famous Lancaster firm, Waring and Gillow, who were better known as cabinet-makers. The memorial was erected, at a cost of £87,000, during the period 1907-09. The building, of neo-classical style, was known variously as The Temple of Fame, Taj Mahal or, simply, the Jelly Mould, can be reached from ground level via ninety-eight increasingly demanding steps, forming a stunning curved staircase. The exterior has five balconies, of varying character and different heights, with the interior consisting mainly of two domes chambers, one above the other. Steps lead up from the main terrace to open loggias at the level of the lower chamber, which is 12.8 metres (42 feet) in diameter and height. The dome is decorated with four large frescoes representing commerce, art, history and science, with four smaller ones describing the seasons. The main terrace is 105.8 metres (347 feet) above sea level, while the top of the domes is 152.4 metres (500 feet) above sea level. Little wonder that, on a clear day, Blackpool Tower, the Isle of Man and the Welsh hills can be seen!

After visiting the memorial in 1909, James and his new wife, Florence, otherwise known as Lord and Lady Ashton, decided to have the building opened without ceremony on the following Sunday, 24 October, 1909. This, despite the fact work was not yet completed on the dome and landscaping around the memorial was still in progress. The cynics suggest Lord Ashton did not want an opening ceremony to clash with the official opening of his new Town Hall, which he also donated to Lancaster, in December of that year.

But for all James's generosity in the town of Lancaster, valued at something like half a million pounds in all, relations between him and the people of Lancaster became increasingly tetchy. His wages policy was under fire, he had running battles with emerging trade unions, having no truck with them at all, and on the political front all was not well. It cannot have helped, either, when many of the gifts of chocolate which his new Lady Ashton had presented personally to every schoolchild to celebrate the opening of the new town hall, were flung back over the wall of Ryelands Park, the splendid location for the family home.

Acknowledgement

I would like to thank Susan Wilson for all her help in the library in researching this article.

11. FROM CONFINEMENT TO COMMUNITY: THE STORY OF 'THE MOOR', LANCASTER'S COUNTY LUNATIC ASYLUM

by Peter Williamson

AS THE YEAR 1999 DREW TO A CLOSE, one of Lancaster's great institutions finally closed its doors for the very last time. From its inception in 1816, until its closure 184 years later, many thousands of people had passed through the long corridors and lofty halls of the Moor Hospital, and its impact upon their lives can never be underestimated.

Changing Attitudes

The first years of the eighteenth century had seen the initiation of tremendous changes in the care and treatment of the insane poor in England. This concern led to an Act of Parliament 'for the better Care and Maintenance of Lunatics, being Paupers or Criminals, in England',[1] which was passed in 1808, being the forty-eighth year of the reign of King George III. This Act gave local Justices of the Peace the power to set up rate-supported asylums for the mentally ill, and the first such institution opened in Nottingham in 1811. There soon followed a rapid expansion of the system 'encouraged by a mounting conviction among reformers that asylums could do more than merely provide a safe refuge for lunatics: they could also cure them'.[2]

In Lancashire, the Court of Annual Sessions met on 1 August 1809, and resolved 'to erect a Lunatic Asylum, or House, for the reception of Lunatics or other Insane Persons' in the County Palatine of Lancaster. A Committee of Justices was subsequently formed, with Sir Richard Clayton as chairman, and they held their first meeting in Wigan at the *Eagle and Child* tavern on 29 August 1809. Their purpose was to take into consideration the provisions of the afore-mentioned Act, for 'the expediency and propriety of providing a Lunatic Asylum, or House of Reception for Lunatics and other insane Persons within the said County'.[3]

Commitment and the Corporation

In 1812, the Committee resolved that 'the asylum be erected in the neighbourhood of Lancaster, on a plot of five acres of land presented to the County Palatine by the Corporation of Lancaster'.[5] In pursuit of this aim, therefore, the Borough offered a parcel of land beside the racecourse on the nearby moor, free of charge. However, contemporary accounts argued that it was also considered an advantage 'to remove patients from the scene of their malady to some situation not too easy of approach for their friends and former associates, whose visits are often found prejudicial'.[5] Adverts were placed in the local paper, the *Lancaster Gazette*,[6] calling for tenders to be submitted for the construction work, to plans drawn up by the local 'architect', Thomas Standen.

Thomas Standen, as noted in the 1816-17 *Lancaster Commercial Directory*, was the 'architect' of the Asylum, but this appears to heave been his only recorded commission as a practicing architect.[7] He was a contractor on the Catholic Chapel in Dalton Square, but this 'slater, plasterer and builder' was declared bankrupt in 1824. The hospital opened on 28 July 1816, with Dr David Campbell as Visiting Physician and Dr Paul Slade Knight as the first Superintendent and Resident Surgeon. He stresses the need for 'good moral and religious characters to act as keepers' (although he himself was later dismissed for his over-use of 'physical coercion and mechanical restraints').[8]

Construction and the Country House Asylum

The design of the hospital was based upon a typical country house of the late Georgian period, being a 'noble pile of buildings (Figure 1),

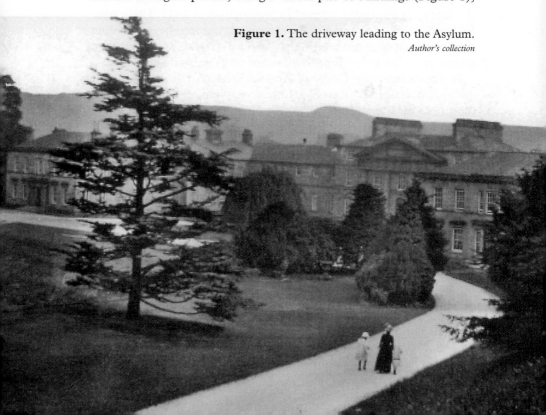

Figure 1. The driveway leading to the Asylum.
Author's collection

with a handsome and stately stone front, ornamented with pillars of the Doric order'.[9] At this time, there was no conception of what an 'asylum' should look like, and the oldest part of the hospital, therefore, could easily have been mistaken for the family residence of some local squire or wealthy merchant. The *Lonsdale Magazine* reported the Asylum to be 'the most magnificent edifice, the Castle excluded, of which Lancaster has to boast'.[10]

The front of the building housed the Superintendent's Office, Nursing Administration and associated staff and servants, with kitchens and stores in the first floor. The patients, meanwhile, lived in wards of galleries running down either side of a central courtyard, which were heated by hot air pumped beneath the flagstones and open fires, despite the obvious dangers. Such features were highly praised, as was the 'almost inconceivable neatness and cleanliness which pervade every part of this immense establishment'.[11] In the first sixty years, patients were admitted, but it soon became obvious that 'the plan of this institution has been but too successful and the building is generally filled with patients'.[12] By 1824, therefore, it was deemed necessary to extend the hospital buildings to the rear, where new wings, to designs by the famous Lancaster architect, Edmund Sharpe, were added.

Control and Confinement
In 1841, Dr Edward de Vitre[13] and Dr Samuel Gaskell wrote the first report on the Lancaster County Lunatic Asylum. Despite acknowledging that their 'enlightened predecessors... lent their best energies in furthering the interests of the institution',[14] it was quite obvious that things were in need to change. This was a period when it was not only the mentally ill who were admitted into asylums. It was believed that women suffered 'a variety of disorders of the menstrual frustration, pregnancy, parturition and suckling which meant they were greatly predisposed to suffer from the exciting causes of insanity'.[15] With such accepted diagnoses it was hardly surprising that mothers of illegitimate children, promiscuous females, and even those who simply 'misbehaved' in the eyes of Victorian society, were often incarcerated.

At the time of the Report, there were 530 patients being 'cared for', including twenty-nine persons 'wearing handcuffs, leg-locks or strait-waistcoats - exclusive of between thirty and forty patients who were chained down during the day-time on seats'.[16] Such constraints had been used for 'idiotic and violent patients, and those of filthy habits,'[17] from when the Asylum opened, although by the time of de

Figure 2. Gallery 5 in the 'Old Side' of the Asylum. *Author's collection*

Vitre's appointment, this system had been abolished. The Report then described the ways in which the patients were now to be treated and cared for (Figure 2), namely through a 'uniform system of kindness, attention, and consideration of their comforts and wants',[18] based on the pioneering treatment of the insane introduced in France some fifty years earlier by doctors Pinel and Esquirol.

Compassion and Kindness

Dr de Vitre was amongst the first to practice modern treatments, and he believed that 'love was the great improver of the idiot. He must be led gently, treated kindly, and shown that those above him were striving to benefit him from a feeling of love'.[19] However, de Vitre was well aware that 'the attendants, who considered their duty finished when they had chained down the patients, would have some difficulty in calling into action the necessary watchfulness, care and ingenuity as substitutes for the instruments of coercion'.[20]

Clothing improved too, including the introduction of non-destructive materials, and the patients' diet now included a beer ration. Occupational Therapy was introduced, as 'the playing of games was deemed important in the welfare of the patient as they stimulated the mind and provided an interest'.[21] Freedom of movement within locked wards became a priority, and the results were immediate and often dramatic, 'one patient who had been rigidly confined for a length of time has since been discharged cured'.[22]

The asylum continued to grow and was rapidly developing into a wholly self-contained community of its own, with farms and allotments, bakeries, sewing workshops (Figure 3), a soda-water bottling plant, as well as the extremely vital laundry. A further wing extended from the back of the chapel, and all around were neat, landscaped gardens, which appear to have developed in piecemeal fashion over the years, as it was recognized that pleasant

Figure 3. The sewing room. *Author's collection*

surroundings could have beneficial and calming effects on disturbed and agitated patients.

Celebrity Guests and Courageous Characters

There was much local interest in the Asylum and the general public were allowed the freedom to roam the wards. This practice was stopped in later years, but not before two popular Victorian celebrities of the day had paid a visit in 1857. The *Lancaster Guardian* of 19 September recorded the event:

> *Mr Charles Dickens: accompanied by Mr Wilkie Collins arrived in this town on Saturday evening from Carlisle, and took up their quarters at the Kings Arms. On Saturday, the two gentlemen, accompanied by the Rev F B Dandy, visited the Asylum and were shown through the principle departments of that well-conducted establishment, and made many enquiries as to its management.*[23]

Meanwhile, the patients' priorities and comforts were far more basic, and fundamental in this process, were the nursing staff. Whether male attendants or female nurses, theses were the front-line troops who had to possess the physical and moral courage to deal with the patients on a day-to-day basis. The need for special people to deal directly with often-difficult patients in difficult circumstances was acknowledged as paramount to the effective treatment of the mentally ill. The 1841 report had also admitted that it was very difficult to find the right people for the job, but desired those whose 'principles and moral character could stand the test of the closest investigation; and above all, he must be able to subject his moral courage to great forbearance'.[24]

Christianity, Churches and the Queen

To help complete the process of creating a normal 'community', a Protestant church, dedicated to St Michael was opened in December 1866,[25] and St Cuthbert's Catholic Chapel was built later. Further extensions were added to the Asylum complex in the following years to accommodate the growing population, so much so, that it was eventually realized another hospital would be advantageous.

Dr de Vitre had long been aware of the 'different needs of the feeble-minded and the insane, a distinction many people were unable to make.' He therefore proposed that a separate hospital be set up, whereby those with 'learning difficulties' could receive special care and training, rather than being incarcerated with the insane in the County Asylum. Although de Vitre had propounded his theories for many years, it was not until he received a donation from James Brunton, a local businessman, in 1864, that plans for the Royal Albert Asylum could begin.[26] Fund-raising was hugely successful, and even included a donation from Queen Victoria. She agreed to become patron, with the result that, in 1866, forty-three acres of land at Greaves was bought to establish the hospital. The Royal Albert began admitting patients in 1870, in the hope that this new institution would relieve the pressure on the Moor, however this was not the case. The rate of 'lunatic' admissions for the County continued to grow, and building yet more wards became a necessity.

Continued Expansion and Cultivation

In 1879, work started on forty-one acres of land across Quernmore Road, known as the 'Lancaster Moor'. The 'Annexe' was opened on 1 March 1883 (Figure 4), with a patient capacity of 825 beds, at a

Figure 4. The 'Annexe'. *Author's collection*

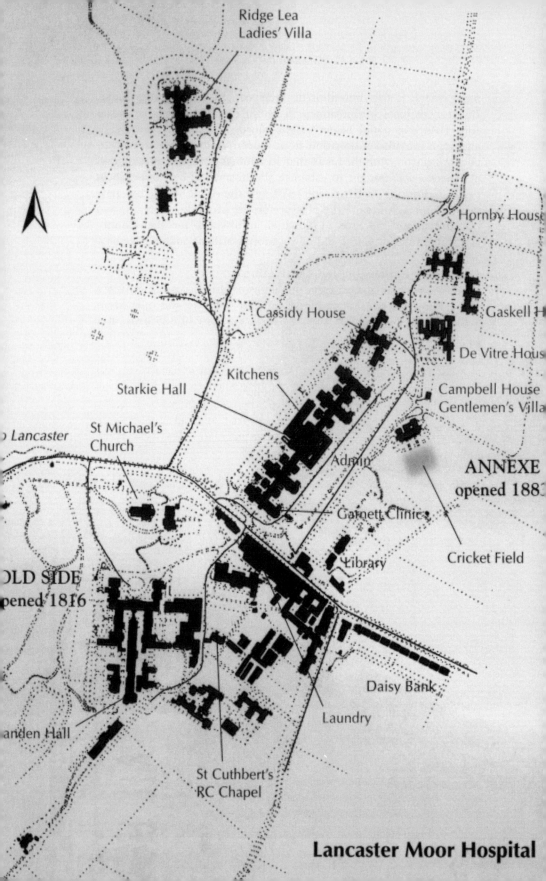

Ridge Lea
Ladies' Villa

Hornby House

Gaskell H

Cassidy House

De Vitre Hous

Kitchens

Campbell House
Gentlemen's Villa

Starkie Hall

Lancaster

St Michael's
Church

Admin

ANNEXE
opened 188

Garnett Clinics

OLD SIDE
pened 1816

Library

Cricket Field

anden Hall

Daisy Bank

Laundry

St Cuthbert's
RC Chapel

Lancaster Moor Hospital

cost of well over £100,000.[27] The design of this grand, if somewhat sombre looking edifice was based very much on Victorian lines of neo-Gothic classicism. It is in stark contrast to the relaxed 'country house' style of the original hospital in 1816.

In 1890, the administration of the Asylum came under control of the Lancashire Asylums Board, when it was enacted that 'if a duly recognized officer of the local Health Authority has reasonable grounds for believing that a person is of unsound mind then he or she is to be sent to the mental hospital'.[28] Similarly, if the Judicial Authority so ordered 'a person not being of unsound mind could still be received into an institution'.[29]

The number of in-patients had risen to 1,833 by 1890, and further accommodation was provided by the erection of several smaller villas around the Annexe. The new satellite wards included Cassidy House (1907), Campbell House (1909), de Vitre House (1912), The Ladies' Villa (1916) and Gaskell House (1938), by which time the patient population was 3,048.[30] The Ladies' Villa (Ridge Lea Hospital) was built in response to wealthy relatives of female patients objecting to members of their families mixing with persons from the lower classes. The Asylum also now owned three farms, where the patients were encouraged to help in the cultivation of crops and in animal husbandry (Figure 5).

Complications and Class Distinctions

Not only were people concerned about the treatment and conditions of the patients, but also they were concerned about the condition of the buildings themselves. The report from 1924 noted that

> the number of institutions having the status of county mental hospital is ninety-seven, and their ages vary from 100 to three years. This diversity complicates our problem, for many of the older ones do not comply structurally with modern requirements. The mental hospital at Thorpe for the county of Norfolk was opened in 1814, and that as Park Prewett for Hampshire in 1921.[31]

Treatment, care and administration were constantly being updated as was the equally important terminology applied to the mentally ill. There was never any intention to offend, as the term used in times gone by were thought to be correct, whilst undergoing constant revision. The 1913 *Mental Deficiency Act*[32] listed definitions of defectives. 'Idiots' were seen as those in whom 'there exists mental defectiveness to such a degree that they are unable to guard themselves against common physical danger'; 'Imbeciles'

Figure 5. Plan of the Asylum. *Author's collection*

were those whose 'mental defectiveness which, though amounting to idiocy, is yet so pronounced that they are incapable of managing themselves or their affairs'; 'Feeble-minded' persons suffered from 'mental defectiveness which is so pronounced that they require care, supervision and control for their own protection, or in the case of children, makes them incapable of receiving education at school'; whilst 'Moral Defectives' 'exhibited mental defectives coupled with strongly vicious or criminal propensities and who require care, supervision and control for the protection of others'.[33]

Cricket Away-Days and Close Contact
Despite the development of more personal units, some patients preferred to make their own re-entry into the community. *The Escape Book*[34] highlights cricket matches as being the optimum time to head for the boundary! On Wednesday, 28 June 1928, one Arthur Murray escaped from the kitchen working party whilst his attendant was particularly engrossed in a cricket match. He made it to Ingleton before being escorted back by the police in the early hours of 30 June.

Under the 1930 *Mental Treatment Act*, a far more liberal approach was materializing, not only in treatment and attitudes, but also in regard to the décor of the wards, sport, entertainment and occupational therapy. The farms employed many patients, as paid work gave the patients more respect for themselves, and encouraged a semblance of normality within this limited environment. Others helped the porters, or the transport unit, and many more worked in the sewing room and laundry. More still were employed by Standen Enterprises, where concrete was used to make all manner of things.

However, occupational therapy was not just limited to work. Patients and staff alike used Standen Hall for therapy through drama. The *Lancaster Guardian*[35] often reported on the annual shows of the Musical Society, and the hospital orchestra was in great demand, especially when the male and female wards came together for some close contact in the 'Thursday Dance Night'.

Cracks and Criticisms
However, beneath the surface, cracks were beginning to appear - literally. Despite the exceptionally elegant patient dining room, Starkie Hall,[36] designed by Waring & Gillow of Lancaster (Figure 6), and a boardroom hung with ornate tapestries, much of the structure was beginning to show signs of age. Surveyors proceeded to visit and examine every building on the whole hospital complex, making

Figure 6. Artist's impression of Starkie Hall dining room, designed by Waring and Gillow. *Author's collection*

recommendations for improvements, and taking photographs to back up their findings. The report was quite damning. They found modern building techniques overlooked, leading to decay and unsanitary arrangements for many patients. Needless to say, it was not only the patients who suffered. The steam heating had many leaks, and 'nurses living in the Nurses' Home suffer discomfort, as studying for certificates can only be done in bedrooms after their hours of duty'.[37]

Overall, the report concluded that the piecemeal growth of the site had led to an awkward layout, poor maintenance, and serious overcrowding, and a thorough rebuilding programme was urgently demanded. However, war intervened, and a new role developed for the Moor. During the Second World War the hospital was part of the emergency scheme whereby naval officers, suffering from mental problems caused by active service, were transferred to Lancaster from Yarmouth. It was at this time that the Superintendent, Dr Silverston, insisted on a far more professional approach, and all nurses and attendants were instructed and encouraged to sit the exams of the Royal Medical Psychological Association, as well as qualifying as State Registered Mental Nurses.

The Commons and a Comprehensive Outlook

The 5 July 1948 saw the creation of a National Health Service in Britain under the guidance of Aneurin Bevan, the Labour Party's Minister of Health. Its purpose was to promote health, to prevent ill health, to treat illness and disease, and to care for those with long-term health needs. However, Bevan himself stressed the fact that, despite it being a revolution in national health care and the envy of the world, the NHS would always be undergoing evolutionary processes.

Ever since the 1950s there had been a gradual shift towards 'care in the community', whereby certain long-term residents were encouraged to live in smaller units within their local community. Meanwhile, the building became a 'Comprehensive Hospital', whereby the acute sick, chronic sick and mentally ill could all be treated under the same roof, which now housed a comprehensive range of facilities, including X-Ray, Pathology, Physiotherapy and Occupational Therapy. In 1958 the Garnett Clinic opened and this contained surgical and neuro-surgical wards, later joined by orthopaedic and ophthalmic units. Gradually over the years, the hospital continued to develop its facilities to include the treatment of general mental illness, a Blood Transfusion Centre, and a School of Radiography.[38]

Cassidy, de Vitre and Hornby Houses became 'Continuing Care' units, and housed long-stay patients and rehabilitation units, whilst a 'Reminiscence Room' was developed in the Littledale Centre. The idea was that souvenirs of bygone days would provide stimuli to trigger off memories and reminiscences of the elderly long-stay patients.

Community Spirit and Crisis Centres
In the latter part of the twentieth century, patients are being 'freed' from the shackles of life within the confinement of an asylum, and encouraged to live more normal lives, under the care and supervision of trained staff, within the community. Instead of a huge institution looking after thousands of patients under one roof, the governing authorities have gradually begun the process of community care for all but the most serious acute cases.

In the 1960s a Community Psychiatric Nursing Scheme was begun, in tandem with a scheme of Boarding Out the less seriously ill former asylum inmates. Much land was sold off to the Home Office who created Lancaster Farms, the Young Offender's Institute, and reductions in manning levels saw a proportional increase in similar facilities within the local area. The late 1980s saw Hostels for residential care appearing in Lancaster, Morecambe and South Cumbria, whilst the local Acute Trusts instigated a rationalization programme whereby non-mental health patients were reclaimed by the RLI and other local general hospitals.

A Community Rehabilitation team was eventually set up to oversee the care of the patients and to organise the staffing of new units. In October 1993 Red Oak Children's Centre was set up in Scotforth, whilst former staff houses on Daisy Bank were used for further rehabilitation. Harvey House, the alcohol unit, moved to new premises in October 1995, and a Crisis Centre was added to the White Cross team in 1996. More flatlet schemes were opened in 1997 and 1998, and complimentary Resource Centres were established at Victoria House in Morecambe, and St Leonardgate in Lancaster.[39]

Closure and Change
By the end of 1999 there were no patients left within the County Asylum on the Moor. The last few patients were re-housed in Continuing Care facilities in Morecambe, Lancaster and Heysham, and the closedown procedure was complete. Ridge Lea Hospital became the active psychiatric unit, and now houses the Acute Clinic, Clinical Psychologists, Admissions area and associated wards.

The original hospital complex, based around the 1816 structure,

Figure 7. The Moor Hospital, 1999. *Author's Collection*

has now been developed as Standen Park, a luxury residential complex, whilst the Annexe, which once housed some three thousand patients, is now standing empty and pondering its future (Figure 7). A whole, self-sufficient community has been slowly broken up and diluted within the surrounding area. Many staff have been saddened by the closure and will always remember how 'the Moor was a buzzing place and full of camaraderie among the staff'.[40] Meanwhile, the former in-mates, patients, clients and users are now living happily within the community, wither in their own homes or in hostel accommodation, and yet still receiving the treatment, care and support they need, through Day Care, Resource Centres and Domiciliary Treatment.

The recent trend has been to place patients, clients and users in

friendlier more beneficial surroundings, as well as to simultaneously redefine the administration of this huge sector of public health. The aim of current NHS thinking is to put patients first, but helping them to become active partners with health professionals in making decisions about their personal treatment,[41] so that they will no longer be viewed as 'inmates if a lunatic asylum', but as ordinary, albeit dependant, members of society.

Notes and References

1. Letter from the Clerk of the Peace's Office, 11 July 1809.
2. Walton, J K, 'The Treatment of Pauper Lunatics in Victorian England', in Scull, A *Madhouses, Mad Doctors and Madmen*, 1981, p 166.
3. *ibid.*, p 167.
4. At its height in 1948, the hospital and associated facilities went on to cover 587 acres.

5. Barwick, C A, *Guide to Lancaster and its Neighbourhood*, Lancaster 1843, p.70.

6. *Lancaster Gazette*, 29 February 1812.

7. His entry in the *Biographical Dictionary of British Architects*, 1600-1840, edited by H M Colvin, states 'though he is described as architect no other work by him has been noted', p.744. In the late Georgian period there was little distinction between builder and architect.

8. Walton, J K, 'The Treatment of Pauper Lunatics in Victorian England', in Scull, A *Madhouses, Mad Doctors and Madmen*, 1981, p.170.

9. Barwick, C A, *Guide to Lancaster and its Neighbourhood, Lancaster 1843*, p.70.

10. Briggs, J (ed) *The Lonsdale Magazine*, Kirkby Lonsdale, 1820, p.471.

11. *ibid.*, p.471.

12. *ibid.*, p.471.

13. In the 1865 *Lancaster Commercial Directory*, Dr de Vitre was recorded as Borough Magistrate alongside James Williamson, father of Lord Ashton, p.45.

14. Report of the Lunatic Asylum for the County of Lancaster, 1841, p.3.

15. Morison, A *The Nature, Cause and Treatment of Insanity*, London, 1848, p.289.

16. 1841 Report, p.3.

17. 1841 Report, p.4.

18. 1841 Report, p.6.

19. 1841 Report, p.6.

20. 1841 Report, p.6.

21. 1841 Report, p.7.

22. Report of the Medical Officers of the Lunatic Asylum for the County of Lancaster, 1846.

23. *Lancaster Guardian*, 19 September 1857.

24. 1841 Report, p.12.

25. *Lancaster Guardian*, 8 December 1866.

26. Roberts, E *The Royal Albert - Chronicles of an Era*, 1992, p.2.

27. Davies and Davies, *Lancaster County Mental Hospital Survey*, 1939, p.8.

28. Matthews, F B *Mental Health Services, 1948*, p.85.

29. *ibid.*, p 78.

30. *Lancaster Moor Hospital 150th Anniversary*, p.18. The maximum-recorded figure was 3200 patients in 1940.

31. 1924 report, p.8

32. 1891, 1908, 1911, 1913, 1919, 1925, 1927, 1930 and 1938 all saw Acts of Parliament relating directly to the treatment of the mentally ill.

33. Matthews, F B *Mental Health Services, 1948*, p.198.

34. Escapes Book, LMH205, Museum of Lancashire.

35. *Lancaster Guardian*, 19 March 1935, reporting in the production of *Ali Baba*.

36. A wonderful artist's impression by W Eccles once hung in the hospital foyer.

37. Davies and Davies, *Lancaster County Mental Hospital Survey*, 1939, p.5.

38. *Moor News*, August 1958, p.8.

39. Information supplied by the Morecambe Bay NHS Trust.

40. *Moor News*, January 1998.

41. NHS Patient's Charter for Mental Health Services, p.2.

12. LIBRARIES OF LANCASTER

by Michael Margerison

THERE HAVE BEEN MANY DIFFERENT TYPES of library in Lancaster since the late seventeenth century. The idea of a single, central, and public library is a fairly recent concept. The current library, on the site of the old police station (Figure 1), was built in 1932 as the commemorative plaque displays on Market Square, and is at the end of a long development process. A process that began in 1695 on Meeting House Lane, and evolved through a number of steps, over a great many years.

Figure 1. The Proclamation of King Edward VII, 25 January 1901. The present library site is occupied by the police and fire stations. *Lancaster Library Collection*

Figure 2. The Friends Meeting House, Lancaster. *Lancaster Library Collection*

Early Lancaster Libraries
The Friends Meeting House Library

It is widely accepted that Lancaster's first library was developed by the Society of Friends. The Society of Friends, or Quakers, began to grow in Lancaster in the 1660s, roughly contemporary with the Great Fire of London. Their principles of hard work and economy helped them to rise to success quickly and, by 1667 they had built the meeting house which stands on Meeting House Lane today (Figure 2). By 1695 they had founded a library for their members. They regarded books as significant for teaching and learning, stressing the importance of reading for their members. During the 1759 annual meeting the Society asked its members to keep a catalogue of books that would be passed on to the library upon their deaths. By 1899 they had collected nearly eight hundred titles, including the journals of George Fox, the societies founder in 1647[1], himself a famous Lancaster man. Many of these titles remain with the Quakers today. This was quite an impressive number, considering the very poor literacy rates.

The operation of the library was very open by modern standards. There was, for example, no set loan period and very few rules. Quakers were allowed to borrow up to two books at a time, and were even permitted to loan them to non-members, although they took responsibility for the books themselves. The collection included, inevitably, many religious items and very little in the way of frivolous works, such as fiction. There were, however, books such as biographies and official papers pertaining specifically to the Quakers. These included Acts of Parliament with a direct relevance to the Quakers.

Amiable Society Library

Sources suggest this Society was founded somewhere between 1768 or, more likely, 1769. It was in line with a number of book clubs opening up around the country at roughly the same time, the Liverpool Book Club had, for example, opened twelve years earlier in 1757. This Society was quite clearly aimed at the upper middle classes. In the beginning, the books were stored in chests and carted around the various meeting places of the Society's members. This was considered, ultimately, unsatisfactory and permanent premises were obtained. Over the years various different buildings housed this growing library. It began at the *New Inn*, moving to shops and homes. At the turn of the nineteenth century, it was housed on Church Street (Figure 3). It ended its days at Nazareth House in Dalton Square, the site of the present-day Town Hall. It was wound

Figure 3. Church Street, Lancaster. *Lancaster Library Collection*

up in 1906, probably due to competition from the new public library. The building was demolished for the building of the New Town Hall.

The members of the Society paid handsomely for their privileges. Members paid up to three guineas to become shareholders in the library, in addition to their one guinea annual subscription charge. Subscribers, who held far less influence, would pay an annual subscription charge of £1 11s 6d. These fees were very high for the period, and would certainly have been prohibitive to the lower classes. In exchange for this vast sum the member was given a medal, an early precursor of the modern library membership card. An interesting fact about the Society is the way in which they administered fines. The librarian was entitled to half the fine, by way of payment for services presumably. However, if they mischarged someone, they would be liable for a fine themselves!

The Society was, in some ways, quite forward-looking in its membership. As early as 1775, it allowed ladies to become members in their own right, a great many years before they received the vote. It was recorded, with some humour, that within three months of admitting ladies the library began to stock the *Matrimonial Magazine*. In many ways there was a good selection of stock specifically tailored to the Society's needs. The library had a wide range of education journals and periodicals, targeted at educated gentlemen of the middle classes. As early as 1807, the library held 2,200 titles, bearing in mind the public library that would open in 1893 only had 2,000. Its stock included a small collection of fiction and a wide variety of non-fiction. When the Society finally closed down in 1906, the year Sir John Fisher completed his revolutionary battleship HMS *Dreadnaught*, and Lord Ashton unveiled his statue in Dalton Square, its shelves held more than 14,000 titles, including some children's literature. The Amicable Society was held in some high regard; on a visit Lord Macauley described it as 'the best outside London'. It had quite a liberal 'open access' system, quite unlike the public lending library at the same point. A closed access system basically means that the books were kept behind closed doors and a borrower had to ask for each title specifically. There was no browsing across open shelves in the public library. The Amicable Society was probably more trusting of its middle class borrowers and could afford to display its books without fear of damage or theft. For the same reason, there were quite a small number of rules.

Newsrooms and Coffee Houses
Before the widespread acceptance of public libraries, these buildings

were centres for the educated man. One of the first of these was the Merchant's Newsroom. Coffee was an expensive and highly fashionable commodity during the eighteenth and nineteenth centuries. The Merchant's was established in 1792, amid the heat of the French Revolution, the very same year that the Republic was proclaimed in France. The Merchant's Newsroom was in Market Street, surviving until March 1929. It served as a meeting house for the educated, where they could discuss local politics and other issues. No doubt in those early days the French Revolution was a regular topic of conversation for these literate gentlemen of the town. Alongside the Merchant's was the Mechanics' Institute Newsroom, established in 1848. This would have catered for the lower, working classes. Newspapers were expensive, 5d in 1836. This may not sound much but it is worth remembering that a soldier in Wellington's army was paid a shilling (5p) a day. The Mechanics' Institute Newsroom was quite separate from its library, being founded some twenty-five years after the library. This is probably because Newsrooms were not especially about reading they were about information. People used them to obtain information regarding current events and developments, things that changed at a faster pace than a book would. In this respect, they were a true forerunner of the modern Public Lending Service with its role as an information provider; not simply a public lending library.

Libraries in the Nineteenth Century
Changing economic and social patterns of the nineteenth century, particularly rising literacy rates, saw a large number of new libraries emerge in Lancaster. Smaller specialist libraries, such as the Medical Book Club, ran alongside newsrooms and coffee houses, the Church of England Instruction Society and the first truly working class library, Lancaster Mechanics' Institute. There was also a legal library owned by the law society, founded in 1838, and a medical book club founded in 1823, which became a library in 1841. This is to mention a few among many others. By the mid 1870s, there were nine separate libraries operating in Lancaster.

The Mechanics' Institute was founded in 1824, and its library opened a year later with 200 books in stock. It was a truly working class library with a very low fee of 6d (2.5p) per quarter. The first of its kind in Lancaster, it steadily rose in size until it was finally amalgamated with the Storey Institute (Figure 4) in 1887, with 14,000 titles in stock. To begin with it was designed for apprentices, and offered classes to educate the young from 1840, in addition to

Figure 4. The Storey Institute, Lancaster. *Lancaster Library Collection*

its lending facilities. Over the years the stock of the Mechanics' Institute grew by inclusion of other smaller libraries, such as the Farmers' Library and the Literary, Science and Natural History Library. In 1860 the stock of the Lancaster Church of England Instruction Society was handed over wholesale to the Mechanics' Institute. Some 1,000 titles, predominantly religious, were added to library stock. This involved changing the Institute's rules, as originally religious issues were considered too controversial for its readers. Many of the original titles were of a more practical nature.

Lancaster's Public Library

The *Public Libraries Acts* of 1850 and 1855 allowed city councils to levy 1d in the £ in addition to rates to pay for a public library and or museum. In 1858 a town meeting put this proposal forward, but it was roundly defeated with only six supporters. Two years later, in 1860, Thomas Johnson published a leaflet advocating a free library with his four page pamphlet Free Library and News Rooms,[2] again this idea was defeated, and it was not until 1892 that the subject was taken seriously by the city's elders. It is worth remembering that a public library was opened in Skerton in 1878, which provided, along with the obvious books, a reading room, newspapers, a common room, and somewhat surprisingly, a billiards room – an invaluable asset for any Victorian public building. Thomas Johnson's pamphlet is an interesting read for anyone interested in Victorian history, as it is so characteristic of the period:

> *The great mass of lads that saunter about our streets have not a home where they can read comfortably. And yet among them there is a desire, more or less strong, for intellectual improvement*

and he ends with a truly Victorian statement,

> *I hope that the meeting of the burgesses may be conducted in a truly British spirit of fair play, and all arguments on both sides calmly stated, listened to, duly weighed, and honestly decided upon.*

Sadly, his eloquent words had fallen on deaf ears, and it is not until 1892 that the campaign picks up speed. On 12 November, an article was published in the *Lancaster Guardian* outlining the details of a possible library, and on 19 December a public meeting was held to discuss the issue. Four days later, a public ballot was held – 2,822 in favour, 550 against and a staggering 1,173 spoiled papers. The main reason for this seems to have been the failure to sign in these early days before a truly anonymous ballot. On 25 January 1893, the

Public Library Act was officially adopted by Lancaster City Council. In July the reading room opened, and on 11 September the Lending Library opened carrying a stock of 2,000 books; a paltry number when compared with the Mechanics Institute's 14,000, but for the first time the people of Lancaster were able to borrow books for free.

Originally, the public library was held at the Storey Institute, which had been generously donated by Sir Thomas Storey shortly after the Council had adopted the Act. The building, which still bears the same name today, proved too small to accommodate the rapidly growing library stock and the demands of its growing readership. The 2,000 titles of 1890 had grown to nearly 27,000 by 1918, and the town's population had grown from 31,000 on the 1891 census to 41,000 in 1911. In 1904 a four-floor extension was added to the original building, paid for by Sir Thomas Storey's son, Herbert. In 1924, an application for a new building was made, but this was not approved until 1930. In 1932, the central public library on the corner of Market Square was finally completed (Figure 5). The official opening was held on Wednesday, 4 May 1932 in the presence of his worship, Mayor Proctor and the Earl Crawford and Balcarres along with the other members of the Storey Institute and library committee. The building originally included, in addition to Lending (Figure 6), Reference and Children's Library, a 52 foot long lecture hall (Figure 7) and a fifty-seven-foot long reading room. The total cost of the buildings, including furniture and fittings, cost £14,300, a handsome fee for the contractors, Messrs Robert Thompson and Morris of Queen Street, Lancaster.

Every effort was made in the construction of the new building to fit in with its surroundings of the Co-op and the old Savings Bank. This was also true of the old Town Hall, the building that was both then and now Lancaster's City Museum, a building erected in 1783.[3]

In addition to the Lending Library building, there was a Junior Library (Figure 8) with an entrance on New Street. The entrance was originally the entrance to the Lancaster Savings Bank, and although much of the rest of the building was destroyed the majority of the front was preserved, although it was altered to fit in with the building.[4] In 1953, in the Junior department, the

> *books are arranged round the walls, fiction alphabetically according to author, and non-fiction by the Dewey Decimal Classification Scheme, which is according to the subject of the book. This arrangement is identical to the adult Lending Department and helps to train the children to use the Adult departments in later years.*[5]

Figure 5. The front entrance of the present Public Library, Lancaster.
Lancaster Library Collection

Figure 6. The Lecture Hall (now the Reference library). *Lancaster Library Collection*

Figure 7. Inside the Lending library. *Lancaster Library Collection*

Figure 8. The entrance to the Junior Library in New Street. *Lancaster Library Collection*

Figure 9. Lancaster Library staff in 1954. *Lancaster Library Collection*

In the same year the Public Library proudly celebrated its diamond jubilee. A pamphlet was published, and a small exhibition was opened. In addition there were a handful of lectures on such ripping subjects as 'The Detective Novel' and 'People in Books'. The exhibition was held in the Junior Library with the title 'The Two Elizabeths and their Peoples' (Figure 9).

Almost all of the departments were on the ground floor, with the exception of the Lecture Hall that faced onto Market Square. This room has changed its role and today holds Lancaster's Reference and Local Studies materials. It is worth noting the differences between the front of the old Police Station and the front of the 1932 Public Library, as there has been some doubt about how extensively the site of the old Police Station was altered. A casual glance at the supporting photographs shows that whereas the old buildings clearly had three floors, the 1932 building only has two: the Lending Library and the Lecture Hall (see Figures 1 and 5). Although the 1932 building has some visible similarities to the old buildings, they are entirely different structures. It is obvious that whereas the old Market Square buildings were higher than the adjacent buildings, the 1932 Public Library is lower.

Lancaster Moor Hospital

An interesting sideshow to the development of libraries in Lancaster is the development of a library at the Lancaster Moor Hospital. It began as an experiment in 1947, when a full-time librarian was employed for the first time. The hospital library was to be run as any other branch of the County Library Service; this was the first such arrangement in the country. Prior to that the library had been the responsibility of the chaplain, amongst his other more obvious duties. He did, however, have the help of one of the male nurses. This was supplemented by volunteers during the war.[6] In the end, Kathryn Allsop was appointed, a woman with no great library experience, but with considerable education experience. After a three-week training period in other branches, she took up her post in November.

In 1947, there were some 13,000 books in stock, ranging from the new books, tatty old things and a wide selection of old school textbooks. Of this weary selection, only around 5,000 were considered fit for use. The library had a reading room, organised ward visits and offered a variety of courses in the early days. There were also discussion groups and activities such as a Drama Group and a Music Evening.[7] Sadly, the move towards care in the community and the reduction of institutionalised treatment lead to the eventual closure of the hospital library. The doors closed for the last time on 27 March 1997.

Modern Library Developments

In 1971, Lancaster Public Library took the first bold step into modernity. There was established a Gramophone Record Library as a sub-section of the Public Lending Library. For the princely annual sum of £1.50 you could join the Gramophone Record Library, which entitles you to borrow a single record for the period of twenty-one days for the cost of 10p. In more recent years, this section has been greatly extended, to include all manner of other media such as cassettes, compact discs, videos, CD-ROMs and even DVDs, and is one of the most popular elements of the library. As technology moves ever on, even the Library Service has to come down from its ivory

Figure 10. The Lending Library after refurbishment, December 1999. *Susan Wilson*

tower and embrace change. The current public library offers books and audio-visual media, but also offers internet access, as well as being the first port of call for most aspects of public information. Lancaster Library was refurbished in December 1999. Today's modern library is a long way from its embryonic stages that began in Meeting House Lane in the seventeenth century (Figure 10).

Notes and References

1. Books in the Library of Friends at Lancaster, Lancaster 1899.
2. Johnson, Thomas, *Free Library and Newsroom, Lancaster Gazette* Office, 1860.
3. *Municipal Review,* June 1932, p 248.
4. *Municipal Review,* June 1932, p 248.
5. *Lancaster Library Diamond Jubilee,* Lancaster 1953, p 7.
6. Allsop, K M A *Mental Hospital Library,* London, 1951, p 9.
7. Allsop, K M A *Mental Hospital Library,* London, 1951, p 23.

CONTRIBUTORS

1. LANCASTER CASTLE AND THE FATE OF THE PENDLE WITCHES

Susan Wilson was born and bred in Morecambe, and was educated at Morecambe High School. Susan started work at Lancaster Library in 1983. She gained a distinction in the Library City and Guilds examination and moved into the Reference and Local Studies Department fourteen years ago. She is now joint Local Studies Librarian at Lancaster. Susan has always been interested in local history and she gives many talks on the subject to various groups. Susan is also a qualified Speech and Drama Teacher and a performer on the stage. Susan is a member of the Footlights Club and Morecambe Warblers. She is a Rotarian and enjoys music and swimming. She has recently completed a project that has involved taking photos of Lancaster and Morecambe in the year 2000.

2. CATHOLICISM IN LANCASTER AND DISTRICT

Tony Noble was born in Lancaster, and in his school days had an interest in Family and Local history. Retirement after thirty-eight years work in the Civil Engineering Department of British Rail provided time to develop these interests, particularly in the sphere of post-Reformation Catholicism in North Lancashire, on which subject he has had a number of articles published in the *Journal of the North West Catholic History Society*. This society published in 1999, his updated version of H Taylor's work of 1906 describing the crosses and wells of Lonsdale Hundred. He has also collaborated with Mr J S Hayes on the transcription of the 1757 *Militia Ballot List for South Lonsdale*, published by Lancaster City Museums.

Norman Gardner, MPhil, read North West History and conducted housing research at the University of Lancaster as a mature student. An unemployed former psychiatric nurse and industrial worker, he has published many local history articles. Lancaster born, he has been for many years a Eucharistic Minister, reader, parish worker and organist at St Joseph's Catholic Church, Lancaster. His interests include religion, history, archaeology, music, walking, cycling and counting his grandchildren.

3. THE QUAY TO SUCCESS: DEVELOPING AN EIGHTEENTH CENTURY PORT
11. FROM CONFINEMENT TO COMMUNITY: THE STORY OF 'THE MOOR', LANCASTER'S COUNTY LUNATIC ASYLUM

Peter Williamson moved to Lancaster in 1980, and it was through exploring the local area that he developed a love for the City, the Lune valley and the rich history of the region. Working at the City Museum gave him the opportunity to delve deeper into the area's archives, and this interest culminated in reading History at Lancaster University for which he gained a BA (Hons), followed closely by an MA in Historical Research in 1999. Peter is now a successful freelance writer and local historian, with a particular interest in North Lancashire, although he now lives and works out of West Yorkshire. His Writing Agency works for many varied clients from many diverse industries, but history is, and always will be, his first love. He is currently involved in preparing one book on North Lancashire and another on the Lune Valley.

4. The Rise and Fall of the Stained Glass Trade in Nineteenth Century Lancaster

Suzanne Boutin was born in Chorlton-cum-Hardy, Manchester, and now lives in Bare, Morecambe, with her husband Andre. Before her retirement five years ago, she was an Adult Education Tutor for the Victorian and Local History courses at Morecambe Adult Education Centre. A local historian, she has written a number of articles that have been published. Her article, *The Rise and Fall of the Stained Glass Industry in Nineteenth Century Lancaster* is taken from the  dissertation that she completed for the Local History Diploma Course, at Lancaster University, some years ago. Suzanne is also a member of the Lancaster Family History and Heraldry Society and has recently finished researching into the family history of her Lincolnshire ancestors. She is also a founder member of the Local History Research Group that was commenced two years ago in Morecambe Reference Library.

5. The Lancaster Doctors: Three Case Studies

George Howson was born in Lancaster in 1933. Educated at Lancaster Royal Grammar School and Manchester University, he qualified as a solicitor in 1959. He has spent most of his working life in Lancaster, and has held the position of HM Coroner for North Lancashire since 1979. In 2000, he obtained an MA in History at Lancaster University. He is married with two grown-up children.

6. THE FOUNDING OF GREAVES METHODIST CHURCH

Lois M R Louden was born in what was Lancashire and is now Sefton. After university she taught in schools in Nottingham and Staffordshire. Her PhD was gained from the University of North Carolina at Chapel Hill, and she then returned to England to lecture in the History of Education at Nottingham College and then, for fifteen years, at St Martin's College in Lancaster. Her main research interest is the history of voluntary schools in Lancashire, and she has a number of publications on this topic. She is a member of the Greaves Methodist Church in Lancaster and, at the time of the ninetieth year celebrations for which the material in the article was obtained, she was senior steward.

7. THE DUKE'S THEATRE

Bernard Gladstone was born in 1938 and educated at the Lancaster Royal Grammar School. Between 1960-62 he did his National Service with the King's Own in Kenya, Bahrain and Aden, and worked for Mitchell's Brewery for forty years. His experience of theatre was non-existent until 1974, when his children dragged him unwillingly to see the pantomime at the Duke's Theatre. He was so impressed with this production, that he has seen every play since then, and, in 1983, was invited to become the honorary archivist for the Duke's. His other interests include gardening, watercolour painting, walking, and looking after his two grandchildren.

8. A Spirited Leap into the Unknown

Graham K Dugdale was born in Salford, but now lives in Carnforth, near Lancaster. Much of his professional life has been in teaching at Secondary level where he specialised in geography and history. This resulted in a successful job-exchange scheme with a New Mexico junior high school in the United States where he was accompanied by his wife Ann and his son Stephen. Graham's interest in American history resulted in the publication of two western novels for Robert  Hale. Having taken early retirement from education, he now concentrates on the preparation of walking guides in northern England with a mysterious theme. He is also the resident walks writer for the *Lancaster Guardian*.

9. Some Water-Power Sites in the Lancaster Area

Philip J Hudson, BA., BEd (Hons), M.Phil was born in Bradford and educated at Belle View Grammar, St Martin's College and Lancaster University. Retired as a lecturer in 1995, Philip now lives in Settle where he has a local history publishing and printing business, and is edits *Yorkshire History Quarterly, Lancashire History Quarterly,* and the *Industrial Heritage Journal*. He taught in Lancaster for many years, and was recently  appointed Research Fellow at St Martin's College, researching landscape archaeology and industrial history on the Yorks/Lancs borders. Philip has a particular interest in water-powered sites (keeps the NW Mills database), medieval landscapes, agricultural enclosure and field-systems, has written articles for

Contrebis, Lancaster University's North West regional Studies publications, *Northern Mining, The Local History Journal, Archive,* various local history magazines and several books, including one major work, *Coalmining in Lunesdale.* Currently researching and publishing a series of *'Take a Closer Look at ...'* booklets - titles out include Settle, Giggleswick, and the Wenning Mills.

10. THE GRANDEST MONUMENT IN ENGLAND

Mike Walley is the former editor of the *Morecambe Vistor* newspaper. Now retired after forty-three years in journalism.

12. LIBRARIES OF LANCASTER

Michael Margerison lives in Lancaster, where he works in the city Library. He, like so many other graduates of Lancaster University, has been struck by what many students refer to as the curse of the Pendle Witches. The idea being that the majority of us never leave Lancaster! Currently, Michael is undertaking further study at Manchester Metropolitan University to qualify as a professional Librarian. Michael has two loves in life. The one being a lifelong scholarship of History, both local and military. The other being an eternal friendship with the fruits of Ireland: Guinness. When not indulging in any of the above, he enjoys playing board games, watching movies, and following the highs and (particularly) lows of England's test match cricket.

GENERAL INDEX

Abbey Scar, 37
Abbot, William, 43, 44
Ackworth, 59
African Slave Trade, 30
Aldcliffe, 17, 20
Aldcliffe Mill, 100
Allinson, Robert, 105
Altham, Sir James, 10
Amicable Library, 59, 141
Arthington, Robert, 59
Ashton cum Stodday, 16
Assheton, Colonel, 92
Atkinson, Nicholas, 32

Baldwin, Richard, 9
Baldwin, Robert, 34
Barber, Miles, 29
Barrow, Dr, 53
Barrow, James, 33
Barrowford, 12
Batty, Edward, 15
Belcher, Sir John, 121
Bell, Rev. Edwin, 73
Beverley, Minster, 51
Bibby, Edward, 102
Bibby, James, 103
Bindloss, Robert, 87
Binns, Dr, 54
Birket, Miles, 30
Black Horse Hotel, 55
Bolton le Sands, 13
Bonnie Prince Charlie, 23, 96
Booth Hall Farm, 106
Borwick, 16, 20
Borwick Hall, 87, 86, 88
Bosward, Rev., 66
Bowes, John, 31
Bracken, Dr Henry, 17, 53
Bradshaw, William, 104
Bridge Lane, 64
Brigantes, 7
Brockhole, Family, 19
Bromley, Sir Edward, 10
Brown, Rev. G, 18
Brown, Richard, 23
Brunton House, 64
Bryer, Joshua, 33
Bulcock, John and Jane, 10
Bulfield, Alfred, 48
Butterfield family, 30

Campbell, Dr David, 53, 54,
    55, 56, 57, 59, 124
Campbell House, 131
Case, James, 53
Cassals, Dr, 58
Cassidy House, 131
Castle, 7, 8, 10, 11, 12
Castle Hill, 93
Castle Mill, 108
Castle Park, 53
Caton, 16, 20
Cat Walks, 93

Century Theatre, 77
Chant, Rev., 68, 68, 72
Chattox, 9
Chester, Richard, 14
Cholera, 61
Church of Ascension,
    Morecambe, 44
Church Street, 23, 141
Clarkson, Robert, 38
Clifford, Lord Hugh, 107
Cockersands Abbey, 14, 20, 102
Collins, Wilkie, 128
Conder Mill, 102, 109
Conservative Club, 97
Coulston, Thomas, 23
County Asylum, 55
Cragg Hall Farm, 111
Crawford, Earl, 146
Cromwell, Oliver, 87, 92
Curwen, John C, 55
Custom House, 35, 37
Custom House Alley, 34

Dalton Square, 15
Dalton family, 14, 89
Damside Street, 63
Darlington Family, 91
Davies Farm, 110
Davis, John, 67
Demdike, 8, 9, 10
Denny Beck, 110
Denton, Russell, 80
De Vitre, Edward, 125, 126, 128
De Vitre House, 131
Device, Alizon, 9, 10
Device, Elizabeth, 9, 11
Device, Jennet, 9, 10, 11, 12
Dickens, Charles, 128
Dickinson, John, 106
Dilworth family, 59
Dilworth, Mary, 31
Dimbleby, Richard, 117
Dispensary, 53, 54, 55
Dolphinlee, 17, 20, 109, 110, 111
Duke Street, 34
Duke's Theatre, 75
Dundee, 120

Ellel, 16, 20, 109
Ellel Grange, 45
Emmanuel Church,
    Morecambe, 44

Fenton, James, 29
Fisher, Sir John, 142
Fisher, Joseph, 51
Fisher, Richard, 38
Floral and Horticultural
    Society, 55
Footlights Club, 77
Forsyth, John, 74
Fox, George, 8, 140
Foxcroft, Robert, 32, 35
Freeman, 60
Freemasons, 56
Friends Meeting House, 140

Garnett Clinic, 134
Garrick, David, 76
Gaskell, Dr Samuel, 125
Ghosts, 85, 90
Gibson, Charles, 111
Gibson, George, 29
Gillison, William, 29, 31
Gillow family, 18
Golden Lion Inn, 94
Golgotha, 93
Gorst, Bernard J, 73
Goss, Dr Alexander, 25
Grand Theatre, 96
Gray, George, 33
Great John Street, 15
Greaves (The), 45
Greaves Methodist Church, 63
Gregson, Henry, 23
Gresgarth Home Farm, 109

Halton, 13, 16, 20
Hamilton, Duke of, 19
Hargreaves, Henry, 33
Harley, Edward, 8
Harrison, Allan, 29
Harvey House, 135
Hawarden, Edward, 18
Heathcote, John, 31
Heaton cum Oxcliffe, 16
Helme, John, 33
Helme, Norval, 66
Henry VIII, 8, 14, 93
Hewitt, Katherine, 10, 11
Heysham, 16
Highfield, 17, 20
High Sheriff of Lancashire, 120
Hinds, Thomas 33
HMS Dreadnaught, 142
Hodgson, Albert, 17
Hodgson, Christopher, 74
Hood, Thomas 98
Hornabrook, Rev. John, 66
Hornby, 16, 20, 91
Hornby Castle, 91
Hornby Priory, 93
House of Recovery, 58
Housman, A G, 75
Housman, Rev. Robert, 75, 76

Inman, Charles, 32, 33
Jackson, A W, 79

Jacobites, 8, 23, 33
James I, 12
Jenkinson, Richard, 23
John O'Gaunt's Bowmen, 55
John O'Gaunt's Gateway, 93
Johnson, Christopher, 57, 58, 59

King Street, 18, 34
Kirton, John Lawrence, 74
Knight of the Garter, 93
Knight, Dr Paul, 124

Ladies Villa, 131
Lancaster, 16
Lancaster Agricultural Society, 55

Lancaster Farms, 135
Lancaster Commercial Directory, 124
Lancaster Philosophical Society, 119
Law, John, 9
Lawson, Robert, 29
Leighton, 16
Leyden University, 53
Library, Lancaster, 145, 146, 147, 148
Lingard, Dr John, 19
Literary Scientific and Natural History Society, 59
Liverpool, 27,38
Liverpool Book Club, 141
Lofthouse, Jessica, 89
Lowry, L S, 86
Loyne, 27
Lucy Street, 15
Lunatic Asylum, 123
Lune, 27
Lune Mills, 120
Lune Valley, 90
Lungess Tower, 8
Lythe Brow Mill, 100

Malkin Tower, 10
Manby, Rev. John, 56
Marton, Edward, 29
Marton, Oliver, 29
Marton Street, 34
Martyrs Memorial, 15
Mary Street, 15
Mason Street, 18
Mason Street Mass Centre, 23
Mechanics' Institute, 59, 143, 145, 146
Medical Book Club, 56, 58, 142
Meeting House Lane, 139, 140
Melling, 13, 20, 90
Melling Hall, 90, 91
Merchants' Coffee House, 36
Merchants Newsroom, 143
Methodists, 63
Millington, George, 74
Moor Hospital, 123
Moor Hospital Library, 151
Moor Lane, 64
Morton, Earl of, 8
Moss, Isaac, 31
Music Room, 41
Mytton, Henry, 10

Narr Lodge, 109
Newchurch, 10
Nicholson, John, 36
Nisbett's Knitting Factory, 18
North Western Railway, 22
Nowell, Roger, 9, 10
Nutter, Alice, 9, 10, 11
Nutter, Christopher, 9

Overton, 16, 20

Paley & Austin, 25
Paley, Edward G, 25

Park Hall Survey, 106
Parrington, Thomas, 74
Paslew, John, 8
Peel, Earl, 121
Pendle Heritage Centre, 12
Pendle Witches, 8, 9, 10, 11, 12
Phillipi Club, 55, 59
Pilgrimage of Grace, 8, 14
Poole, 53
Port Commission, 27, 28, 29, 31, 32, 35
Posthlewaite, Thomas, 32
Post House Hotel, 111, 112
Potts, Thomas, 8
Princes Street, 34
Public Libraries Act, 145

Quakers, 16, 53, 59, 140
Queen Street, 34
Queen Street Presbyterian Chapel, 48
Quernmore, 20, 102, 104, 106, 108
Quernmore Forest, 99, 110
Quernmore Park Estate, 20, 45, 107, 108
Quernmore Road, 15, 129

Rawlinson, Abraham, 29
Rawlinson, Thomas H, 32
Redfearn, Anne, 9, 10
Red Oak Children's Centre, 135
Reynolds, Francis, 29
Ridge Lea Hospital, 131
Robert Hall, 20
Roby, Isobel, 12
Roeburndale, 20
Rossall School, 44
Roughlee, 10
Royal Albert Hospital, 129
Ryelands Park, 122

St Anne's, Lancaster, 42, 76
Saint Christopher's, Morecambe, 44
Saint Cuthbert's Catholic Chapel, 128
Saint George's Quay, 27, 38
Saint John's Church, Great Harwood, 44
Saint John's Church, Haslingden, 44
Saint John's Studio, Chapel Street, 43
Saint John's, Lancaster, 45, 48
Saint Leonard's Hospital Mill, 110
Saint Luke's, Skerton, 48
Saint Margaret's Church, Hornby, 92
Saint Mary's, Lancaster, 44, 47, 48
Saint Patrick's Chapel, Heysham, 13
Saint Paul's, Scotforth, 48
Saint Peter's Cathedral, 18, 45
Saint Peter's Church, Burnley, 44
Saint Wilfrid's, Melling, 90

Satterthwaite, Thomas, 29
Scale Hall, 20
Scorton, 20
Scotforth, 20
Scotforth Mill, 100
Seward, Charles, 42
Sharpe, Edmund, 25, 125
Shrigley and Hunt, 43, 44, 46, 48, 49, 51
Silverdale, 16, 20
Skelton, Nicholas, 18
Skerton, 16, 20, 99, 145
Smith, Mrs T D, 67
Springfield Hall, 73
Standen, Thomas, 124
Stodday (Ashton with), 16
Storey, Thomas, 146
Storey Institute, 143, 144, 146
Stout, William, 53
Sulyard Street, 63, 64, 66
Sulyard Street Choir, 72
Sun Street, 41
Swarbrick, James, 8
Sweeney, Councillor Winifred, 79
Syon Convent, 14

Tatham, 16
Thompson, James, 32
Thurnham, 16, 17, 20
Thurnham Hall, 88, 89
Touchet, Thomas, 31
Trinity Methodist Church, Clitheroe, 44
Tunstall, 16, 20
Turner, Charles F, 51
Typhus, 55

University, 76

Victoria, Queen, 129

Waring and Gillow, 122, 132, 133
Warton, 16
Warwick, Kathleen Amy, 73
Webster's Farm, 107
Well Tower, 7
Wesley, John, 63
Westham Street, 64
Whalley, Dr Lawson, 59, 60, 61
Whitaker, John, 32
White, Henry, 34
White, Lady, 88
Whittingham, Richard, 108
Whittington, Thomas, 88
Williamson, Henry, 32
Williamson, James, 117, 120
Williamson Park, 119, 120
Willow Mill, 110
Windmill Hill, 33
Winkley, Rev William, 18
Witchcraft, 8, 12
Worswick family, 19
Wyresdale, 20

Yealand Conyers, 19,20